LORD OF THE SUPERNATURAL

Tricked into an Occult and
Rescued by the Holy Spirit

MATTIA LAJUAN HARRIS

authorHOUSE®

AuthorHouse™
1663 Liberty Drive
Bloomington, IN 47403
www.authorhouse.com
Phone: 1 (800) 839-8640

Published by AuthorHouse 09/06/2018

ISBN: 978-1-4634-1998-1 (sc)
ISBN: 978-1-4634-1999-8 (e)

Library of Congress Control Number: 2011911034

Print information available on the last page.

Any people depicted in stock imagery provided by Thinkstock are models,
and such images are being used for illustrative purposes only.
Certain stock imagery © Thinkstock.

This book is printed on acid-free paper.

CONTENTS

ACKNOWLEDGMENTS

DADDY—

The one that I adore. My true and divine love, Adonai. Without your love for me, I would still be bound and tormented by Satan.

You have unleashed me from the plan that Satan had for my life. You have taught me the skill of remaining dedicated unto you. I bless you for teaching me that love and forgiveness are priceless gifts. As you have given these gifts unto me, I shall also give them unto others.

You have comforted and embraced me during my sorrows and discomfort to change. You have helped me to understand the lifestyle of holiness according to the gospels. I will always give you glory and honor above all others.

JESUS

I thank you for the sacrifice that you made for all of humanity. I am grateful that you lived a life that I can use as an example. A life that is pleasing to our LORD.

HOLY SPIRIT

You have taught me so much and I am grateful. I thank you for your patience and kindness. Thank you for never giving up on me, even when I wanted to give up on myself. I love you dearly.

To my mother and father, I thank you for giving me life!

OTHERS

There are so many others that I would like to acknowledge but find it wise not to. My spiritual walk has been both uncommon and horrific and for reasons of privacy I will not. To you all, know that I love and appreciate you immensely.

INTRODUCTION

For many reasons Christians struggle during their faith journey. Certain situations cause them to feel unwanted and unfit to be a part of the body of believers. They have spiritual experiences that are not typical for the average Christian believer. The Christians I am describing have supernatural and paranormal experiences which they cannot explain. They struggle alone in confusion and become trapped by their experiences. Due to pride and shame, they suffer in silence. The silence leaves them feeling abandoned by the LORD and his church.

When some Christians experience angelic encounters, they do not understand how to share this experience effectively. They fear being ridiculed and labeled demonically possessed or insane. This can be a lonely experience. Based on my personal experiences as well as the experience of those whom I have counseled, there is only one option. This option is to leave the church and single handily seek out their own answers for why these experiences occur.

It is never their intention to leave the LORD or Jesus the savior of the world. What is intended is to remove themselves from the discomfort that takes place within the walls of the church which becomes unbearable.

My reason for writing this book is that the Spirit of the LORD requested something from me. He asked me to come out of the closet concerning my truth of the spiritual realm. In sharing my experiences of spiritual ignorance, it is my prayer that you not suffer as I have.

Seeking my spiritual identity led me onto a path of unsafe meditation and deep breathing exercises that over time led me into the worshipping of idols. My result, I lived through a long season of spiritual darkness. Try listening attentively to your loved one when they are speaking with you concerning spiritual experiences. Do what you can to assist them in their journey. In doing so, they will not feel secluded in their experiences.

Satan has plans to entice your children into joining his army. First, he needs to make them believe that they do not belong to the LORD. He needs to make them feel unloved by the LORD. Satan needs to make them feel as though they do not belong in the church growing, learning, and then serving along with the others.

CHAPTER 1

ANGELIC ENCOUNTER

I met the Holy Spirit for the first time when I was a very young child. Possibly four years or five years of age. There was a day that I recall him kneeling near me while I sat on the bedroom floor near the window facing the garden and farm animals.

He spoke to me concerning a game that I knew, follow the leader. I was to follow him and do what he asked me to do. To say what he asked me to say and to follow him to the places in the yard and in the house as he asked me to. I was to say to my family members exactly what he asked me to say and I was only to say his exact words. It was an easy thing to do. So I did.

Angelic encounters were not uncommon for me. I recall falling through the hallway floor as a child. I believe my first angelic encounter began when I became intrigued with my grandfather's construction of the floor vents in the house.

My grandfather built his home from the ground up. I loved to watch him pour cement and place the bricks in place one by one. During one of his home projects, I decided to find out more concerning the hole in the center of the hallway floor.

My curiosity got the best of me. I wanted to know if my foot would fit in the hole and what would happen if it did. When the opportunity presented itself, I took it. My grandfather removed the metal frame from around the vent and walked away.

When no one was looking, I succeeded in placing my foot in the hole. The hole was so big that my entire body fell through.

While falling through the vent I encountered something that felt fluffy. Today I understand this fluffy texture to have been insulation. While falling, I landed in the wings of an angel. Once caught, the angel walked me over to the staircase and placed me gently on the cold hard cement floor.

I recall the sound of water running onto the basement floor. Immediately my attention was drawn to the loud and hectic sound of people running down the basement stairs. They sounded like a herd of cattle. "Oh my God! Are you alright my family screamed?

Once they reached my location they began tugging at my arms and legs. They were checking for broken bones. While all of this was taking place, I remember thinking to myself, "*I am okay, but you are the ones who are hurting me*".

I was very prophetic as a child. Very intuitive and sensitive to the things of the LORD. The Holy Spirit spoke clearly so I could understand him. The messengers of the LORD whom I know to be his angels gave me clear messages to relay to others. Once the message was relayed, I would go back to play time as usual which consisted of digging in the dirt and making mud pies, playing with the animals or my toys.

I understood the angels of the LORD to be my babysitters since they carefully watched over me. I had a great relationship with the Holy Spirit. He taught me how to converse with him. He treated me as a friend. Being a child, I felt as though we were best friends. I knew of Jesus, but I was not as close with him as I was with the LORD, Holy Spirit, or the Angles.

Jesus was not around as much as they were. He only came around in the case of an extreme emergency. A life-threatening or lifechanging event would cause him to appear. I knew that Jesus was an important part of my life, but I did not have a full understanding of his significance.

The angels of the LORD were easier for me to figure out. They were with me daily. They were my safety keepers who were never overbearing but available whenever I was in need.

An experience that I had enlightened me to the LORDs concern for our smallest desires. At this time, I was old enough to walk to the store without being accompanied by an adult.

My friend asked if I would accompany her on an errand. We were to go to the corner store to make a purchase for her mother. It was a summer day and we both wanted ice cream but neither of us had money.

As usual the angels of the LORD were along side of me as I walked. My friend and I discussed our desire to have ice cream. We discussed the flavor of ice cream we would purchase if we had the money. We spoke about the ice-cream in such detail that I could just about taste it.

I was making a request within my heart and soon after I saw coins fall out of the angel's hand and heard the clinging sound as they landed on the sidewalk. I knelt down to pick up the coins and showed them to my friend. We began jumping up and down with excitement because we were able to purchase the ice cream that we had been hoping for.

I shared just about everything with my friend. She knew of my supernatural experiences, but I wanted her to understand what I had been experiencing. I wanted her to be more than an observer. I no longer wanted to be alone in my experiences. Having a friend who understood would have been helpful.

During this time of my life I noticed not only the angels of the LORD watching over me, but other spiritual beings that were not sent of the LORD. Those not sent of the LORD lurked around but never attempted to speak to me. They were ghostly in appearance. They hung around the house gathering in circles and traveling through the air.

I noticed a difference between the two types of spirits. The angels of the LORD assigned to me had sharp defined human facial features. Some of the other spirits had human features but were transparent.

As a child I was determined to explain to my mother what was happening to me. I hoped that she would one day listen and help me to make sense of it all. Busy with life and probably believing that I was just a child with an imagination running wild, she brushed my statements off and simply said, "That's nice".

One afternoon, I attempted to point out the location and appearance of my angels to a group of neighborhood friends. They too were unable to see them. I realized that angels and the happenings of the spirit realm were not things that everyone could see or understand. I found myself alone and misunderstood.

I wanted to talk about the spirit realm. I wanted others to notice the things that I noticed and to be as excited about them as I was. When it did not happen, I came to accept that I was different from other children that I knew.

CHAPTER 2

PROPHECY UNACCEPTED

My grandfather had no problem with my intimate relationship with the LORD. What he did have a problem with was my receiving messages from the Holy Spirit or the angles of the LORD. There came a time when my grandfather finally had enough of my messages and demanded that I stop relaying them.

He did not want me to tell him any messages concerning him. My grandfather knew I had no control over my encounters with the Holy Spirit. Even so, he was uncomfortable with me telling him things that were to come. He expressed to me in a loving yet stern way that I was to stop immediately.

I wanted to obey my grandfather, but I was unable to stop repeating the LORD's messages. It was important that I did what I was told so I continued. My prophecies and predictions continued as I followed instructions. In aggravation, my grandfather put his foot down. He made it clear that I could no longer tell him what the LORD said.

One day my grandparents and I were preparing for a drive. The three of us were sitting in the car prepared to leave when I received a message. This angel came to the right side of the car and sat down beside me. "Tell your grandfather that one of his family members will be shot," the angel said. Then the angel told me who would be shot.

Immediately, I repeated what I had been told. As I was explaining the details to my grandfather, I was interrupted by his loud yells. "Stop it! Stop doing that, you little thing you!" he screamed. My grandfather was from Opelika, Alabama. His terms of endearment were quirky and might be misunderstood by outsiders.

Until I was almost a preteen, my grandfather would squeeze my cheeks and tickle me while he said, "I love you, you little thing you," or "you are just the sweetest little thing, I just don't know what to call you."

On this day when my grandfather called me "you little thing you," he was angry. There was no term of endearment here. When he yelled at me using those words that he used to be kind, I was heartbroken because he was not happy with me. For my own sake I remembered how dear I was to his heart even in his anger.

It was hard for my grandfather to watch me go through these spiritual experiences and not be able to understand them. It was not until I became an adult that I was told that my grandfather did not believe in women preachers, therefore he scolded me for prophesying to him.

After I repeated what the angel said concerning a shooting death of a family member, my grandmother scolded me. Looking back towards the seat where I was seated she said "Tee, you stop that". I began explaining that my angel gave me the message, so I had to say it.

Suddenly my aunt came to the front door. She yelled toward the car for my grandfather. "Dad," she said. "It is the telephone, and it is for you." She said someone in the family had been shot, and she named the person.

Upon hearing her words my grandfather cried out several times, saying, "Oh God!" He opened the car door to get out of the driver's seat. He was trembling and shaking and crying out to the LORD.

Seeing my grandfather in so much pain made me realized that I did not want to relay messages for the LORD anymore because I did not want to cause people to cry.

I believe I was given the message for my grandfather so he could be better prepared for the news that his loved one had passed. Perhaps it was a way of helping ease his pain. I do not know why I was asked to tell him.

Maybe if he had listened to me when I began attempting to tell him, out of curiosity he would have called the family to check on them. If he called them maybe the shooting might not have happened. If he had listened to me and called the family, the LORD might have used him to help our relative avoid the incident that led to the shooting death of a loved one.

Either way, once my grandfather heard the news he was crushed. I watched my grandfather walk down the concrete steps and into the house to answer the telephone. I sat quietly in the car with my grandmother and the angel of the LORD that delivered the message to me.

My grandmother was aware of what was taking place in my life. I know this because, after the heartbreaking news about the shooting she called for me to come into the kitchen. She was sitting in the chair near the telephone that was mounted on the kitchen wall. She asked me to come closer to her. She did not want others to hear our conversation.

Once I was close to her she said, "Stop telling people what is going to happen to them. Everyone can't handle it." She told me stories about the old days. She said talking like this would cause people to believe that you are a witch. She warned me that parents would not allow their children to associate with me out of fear.

It was then that she opened her heart and shared her childhood experiences with me. My grandmother's prophecies caused people to treat her as an outcast. She said that she only told them what the Holy Spirit said but it was not accepted.

She said that she eventually shut down and stopped relaying messages for the LORD. She encouraged me to do the same thing. She asked me to come to her from that point on anytime that I received a message from the LORD and she would listen. I took her advice. For a while, I kept the messages between my grandmother and myself, the LORD, Holy Spirit, angels of the LORD, and Jesus.

CHAPTER 3

THE MISUNDERSTOOD CHURCH

My immediate family belonged to a Baptist church. The mixed messages that I received while attending this church caused me to feel uneasy and spiritually restless. I felt as though I did not belong in the church due to the spiritual influences that I encountered.

The ministers were excessive in their behavior of pointing fingers and staring at people as they drove up in their cars. Many of the members were rude, mean, and judgmental. I was told that we were going to the house of God to worship. To me the church never felt like a house of God.

As a child, I understood the LORDs heart to be that of kindness. He expected me to follow directions and behave myself. My witness of God was that he was fair, only in the church I was not treated fairly. The LORD did not treat me the way that the people in church did. Because of my positive experience with the LORD, I did not understand how I could go to a place that claimed to be his house and be mistreated.

Terrified is the word that best describes my feelings as I was driven into the church parking lot. Anxiety filled my heart as I opened the car door and walked toward the church. Today, I recognize these actions were set up by Satan who was placing strongholds upon my life concerning the house of the LORD.

The church was supposed to be a place where I would learn how to properly worship and adore our Lord Jesus but I did not. What I did learn was how fear enters the heart. I learned to be afraid of the judgement that I would receive once I walked into the doors of the church. This made it difficult for me to enjoy attending church services. My heart became bitter concerning the church. I did not understand why my grandfather insist that I be present. Being a child in this church I learned nothing.

One Sunday my grandmother allowed me to wear my favorite dress to church. I was excited! I looked in the mirror and I seemed to be okay. I wore my hair in two pony tails. I wore my black patent-leather shoes with folded down socks with ruffles on them. I adored my outfit and picked it out all by myself. My grandmother said that I looked good and that all my colors matched. I went to church expecting to enjoy Sunday school with the other children, but I did not. As I walked up the staircase to enter the sanctuary, some of the older women were in a group talking. They looked at my dress and shook their heads in disapproval.

My typical Sunday morning routine went something like this. As I entered the church, directly in front of me was the staircase that led to the sanctuary. Once I climbed the stairs to enter the sanctuary, my terror began. As I walked to my seat from the distance, I was greeted with looks of disapproval from the older ladies who wore big hats. The teenagers and children who were related to the ladies with the big hats were just as mean. I felt awful going to church. The looks I received were more than simple stares, they were judgement.

It appears a group of hat-wearing ladies investigated my attire from head to toe every Sunday. This was discouraging for me as a child. They began by looking at my shoes and slowly worked their way up until our eyes met. It would be at that very moment in which something seemed to pierce my very soul. They would then shake their heads slowly with looks of disgust and ridicule. One by one they would turn around and face the pulpit.

Growing up in this church truly discouraged my heart. Each time I stepped foot on the church grounds, I felt as though I did not belong there. I did not understand how this could be the same church that served and loved the LORD.

Eventually my grandmother stopped going to church because of the negativity. There were church disputes every Sunday between the members and leadership. My grandmother said that she could serve God better at home. I hated to see her stay at home when we all left for church. I wanted to stay at home with her. I too believed that I could serve God better at home, playing with the animals in the yard. Growing up on the farm I was responsible for taking care of the animals. I had a goat, dogs, cows, chickens, horses, pigs as well as plants that I could water.

I would rather have been home on the farm. Although my grandmother stopped going to church, my grandfather remained a member. He said that he was going to stay where the LORD was leading him. In Sunday school we were taught that God was love. If love was there, I never experienced any of it. Bickering about who was in authority and gossip went swiftly through the church, and it came from the ladies who were supposed to set the example of holiness. Drama and judgement came from these ladies, who were supposed to represent the love of God.

During the service, there were discussions concerning which church members were really shouting under the power of the Holy Ghost and which ones were faking. Discussions about nonsense took place even while the preacher was preaching. So much for the ladies respecting the LORDs word. My young spirit was troubled in a great way while I spent time in that place they called a house of God.

I was confused because I had been told that I could not speak while the pastor was preaching. But the talking, gossiping, and pointing of fingers during the church service were distracting to me. I began to believe that visiting the house of God was not really about God or his love for us at all. Instead, it seemed to be about the ladies who came to church wearing huge hats and judged everyone who did not dress like they did. It seemed to be about the men and women who stood outside the church judging the cars that people were driving.

The message preached in my youth was neither effective nor strategic. While he was preaching, my pastor made crazy breathing sounds that made me afraid that he would not make it through the sermon without being rushed to the hospital. I thought the man was dying. This was frightening to me. He made crazy sounds that caused me to believe that he was having an asthma attack. I had asthma as a child, so I could relate to his struggle to breathe. I was afraid for him and did not understand why no one was helping him.

He would say a few words and then drink some water or juice. He yelled and screamed the entire sermon. The people would scream, "Amen, Pastor!" I could not understand a word that he said, but the words "preach on Pastor, preach!" rung through my ears throughout the service.

The pastor would start out saying, "And Adam … huh … was with Eve … huh … And yes! … Yes!" The people would yell. Then the pastor would yell. He'd walk across the pulpit with large steps and then bend over, wiping the sweat from his forehead.

I was not happy at this church. It appeared as though the pastor never completed his sentences. I was always on edge, waiting to hear the rest of the story so that I could make some type of meaning out of it. The pastor would wipe his forehead with the handkerchief and then go and sit down. The choir would sing, and the offering would be collected. It was time to go home. It was such a waste of my time.

That type of preaching was all that I knew. When I went to Sunday school the judgement was similar. The children in Sunday school were being raised by the very individuals upstairs who were both mean and judgmental. The children were like their parents. There was no winning in that atmosphere of ridicule. I can only imagine that it did not help when I attempted to tell my Sunday school teacher what the Holy Spirit had asked me to share with her. Her reply was for me to go sit down and color.

By my early teens, I was totally frustrated and decided to stick to what I knew. I knew the LORD in my own personal way. I had experiences and encounters with him. I did not have biblical understanding. I relied upon what I did have, and that was love. I wanted to be where I was loved. I wanted to be with my spiritual family.

In my late teens I felt my heart calling me away from the building of the church to learn who I was. To find my purpose in life. I knew deep in my heart that I did not belong in the church. Something greater, something deeper was calling me to a greater understanding. It was then that I decided to leave the church in search of what was missing. I was missing the LORD in a greater way.

CHAPTER 4

CANCER SCARE

Several years passed, and I became comfortable not being a part of any church. I had peace and happiness in my life. No more being discouraged by my church family. I was free from judgment, ridicule, and sermons that left me feeling empty and confused.

One afternoon, the mailman brought a letter that stated it was time for my yearly checkup. I made my appointment and left it at that. The day of my appointment was sunny and bright. I had my exam, paid my bill at the receptionist desk, and headed out the door to enjoy my day. Soon after, I received a telephone call from my doctor's office and then from my doctor. He said that my test results were in and that he wanted to discuss my test results in person. From the sound of his voice I knew that it was urgent.

He said he needed to see me in his office right away and that it could not wait. I asked if I was okay. He would not respond to my question over the telephone but made it clear that he needed to see me in person. Once there, instead of taking me to the examination room as usual he led me into his private office. I will never forget the words that came out of his mouth: "Ms. Harris, you are headed toward stage four cancer. I'm going to do everything that I can to save your life."

Immediately, I became sick to my stomach with both fear and grief. My doctor took me to an examining room where he conducted more tests. He confirmed that he had been correct the first time. I was truly headed into stage four cancer. The only thing that came to my mind was who would take care of my children.

I had two small children and I wondered who was going to raise them in the way I would. I had planned to enjoy my summer with my family. Circumstances wanted me to begin planning my funeral. The doctor insisted that my treatment of chemotherapy begin immediately. I wanted to avoid chemotherapy altogether.

I got off the examining table and together my doctor and I walked to the receptionist's desk, so I could schedule an appointment to begin my treatment. I walked out of the office in tears. I was devastated as I sat in my car wondering what I would do. I decided within my heart, for the sake of my children that I would not accept this death sentence.

I decided to stay in denial and avoided my doctor's telephone calls. When he couldn't reach me, he called my mother and the one friend I'd listed on my emergency contact form. My doctor demanded that they ask me to call him immediately. Whenever I went to visit my mother and friend they would look at me quite strange as though I had been keeping a secret concerning my health. When they brought it to my attention, I responded to them nonchalantly telling them what they wanted to hear which was that I would call the doctor back.

When the doctor continued to call my family, they wondered why I wasn't taking his calls more seriously. Eventually my mother threw her hands up and blurted out, "What's wrong with you?" I replied by shrugging my shoulders and then ended the conversation by saying that I was all right.

I began feeling anxious and felt compelled to go to church. I remembered being a young girl and hearing the old folks say that whenever you are in trouble, just run to the LORD. Thinking about it for a short while, I concluded that I had nothing to lose since I was sick and dying anyway.

It had been a long time since I had walked through the doors of a church. I submitted to the Holy Spirit and asked him to please lead me to the church that he wanted me to attend.

One Sunday morning I woke up with a mental image of the church that I was to attend. I bathed, got dressed and left for church. I did not attend my family church but instead was led to a church in New Haven Connecticut where my aunt and uncle were members. The minister spoke very well. I understood his sermon clearly from beginning to end. The teaching made sense and I decided to go back again on the following Sunday. The lesson was so well taught that I felt a good friend of mine would enjoy the pastor's sermon as well, so I invited her to come with me.

My friend accepted my invitation. Together we went to the church and enjoyed the service greatly. Not long after being there an angel of the LORD revealed part of himself unto me. Right in the middle of the aisle about four rows ahead of me stood a huge angel. He stood there and in his hands, was a large gray bucket. The angel seemed to have white gloves on because they were covered in a white cloth and his fingers were not exposed.

The angel tossed the contents of the bucket forward and onto me. When the contents were tossed towards me from the bucket it looked like confetti, but once it landed upon me it was a clear liquid that I assumed was water.

I thought to myself, *What in the world just happened to me?* I looked around to see if anyone else had noticed. Everyone was sitting in the church, listening to the sermon as though nothing had happened.

Within seconds the angel did it again, just like he had before. I was drenched from head to toe. I turned to my friend and said, "Look at me!"

In disgust, she scooted her bottom over to the left, moving away from me and the wet wooden pew. In a snappy voice, she said "What is wrong with you? Did you wet yourself here in church? The floor is wet, and you are soaked."

After she spoke, the angel doused the clear liquid upon me for the third and final time. This time the liquid also splattered on my friend. The two of us were sitting in church, wet with an unknown substance from the neck down. With the tone of voice that showed both fear and frustration she said, "Girl, let's go! You always have something going on with you." She repeated the words again, "There is always something!" She got up and walked toward the door.

I got up and followed her out. In a calm voice, I said to her, "You didn't smell anything foul, so you know that it is not urine." She did not respond but only shook her head, and together we walked toward the door while she wiped the wetness off her body.

I opened the church doors and together we walked out. The sun beamed upon my face, and immediately my burdens lifted. I was filled with an awesome overwhelming feeling of peace. As the days passed, I was consumed by feelings of hope. I no longer feared death. After about a week of this newfound joy, I decided to stop running from my doctor's telephone calls. I wanted to face my medical condition head on. I made an appointment with my doctor's office to begin chemotherapy

Once I arrived, it was apparent that the doctor was furious. He lectured me on the damage that I might have caused by not receiving treatment in a timely manner. He said that I could have reduced my chances for a full recovery. He wanted me to take more tests to see how far the cancer had spread, and I agreed.

Once he received the test results, he had a look of shock and disbelief. He had the nurse walk over to the laboratory that was in a building next door to verify my results. The results indicated that I was now cancer free. The doctor's demeanor changed, and he gave me a clean bill of health right there on the spot.

With a burst of excitement, he interrogated me: Where have you been? What have you been eating differently? What have you done differently since your last visit? Have you gone anyplace that you have never been? My response was that I hadn't eaten anything different. I had done the same things I had always done. The only thing that had changed was that I started going to church.

He said to me, "Whatever you've been doing, keep doing it. Ms. Harris, you are in better health than you were the last time I saw you." He told me that he was happy for me. He said that things like this just don't happen. He asked me if I minded giving him more tissue samples. I told him that I did not mind.

With a look of amazement, the doctor clipped some tissue from my insides and then sent me on my way. I left the doctor's office even more at peace. It had been confirmed: I was going to live. In the elevator I cried, but when I got to my car and sat down and a mental lightbulb went off in my head. I realized that I had received my healing from that angel of the LORD at the church. The one who tossed the water on me at the church where my aunt and uncle attended. I then understood what that incident was all about. It was a miracle from the LORD. I was very thankful for my healing and continued to attend services at the same church in New Haven.

I felt that if I stayed that eventually I would learn of the LORD biblically. Even with the right attitude my dedication to learning at this church was short lived. There were some incidents that took place that discouraged my regular attendance. Things began to happen to me when I was at church and I could not understand what was taking place. Whenever I asked questions concerning my experiences while at the church I received no answers. It seems that people were just too busy to help me understand. I was being over looked and in my opinion spiritually neglected.

Strange things began happening. There were times when I would begin jumping around in circles while crying and full of joy. When I asked members of the church about this they did not answer me. They were just too busy, and I fell through the cracks. I felt as though I was in a church with people who ignored me and my need for spiritual enlightenment. Nobody came to me and asked me if I understood what had happened to me. No one explained to me what was taking place, or why I was jumping around in circles and crying.

Today, I realize the reason for my jumping up and down. I now know that I had been over taken by the Holy Spirit. At the time I did not understand and since there was no one there that was willing to teach me, old pain from being hurt within the walls of the church had crept in and I no longer wanted to be a part of any church.

Feeling lost from the lack of church wisdom but not from my spiritual experiences, I decided. Leave the church and all its disfunction and continued in my personal relationship with the Holy Spirit. In doing this I felt sure that I would eventually find out who I was and why I was different.

CHAPTER 5

LEAVING CHRISTIANITY

It was now summer. My heart was reminded of my childhood friend. It was a long time since I had been to my hometown and even longer since I had seen her. I decided to go and visit.

After spending time with her I went for a walk to enjoy the sites and view all that I notice had changed since I had last been home. In the past I had enjoyed the view of the Connecticut river. I used to sit on the bench and watch the boats gather and set sail. The restaurant would have live bands playing. Families walked around, and couples held hands at the river. Blankets would be laid out and loved ones would sit around. It was a nice place to go.

After sitting for a while, I decided to go to the baseball park. I had some good childhood memories of the baseball park that was on East Main Street. while walking I met up with an old childhood friend. He asked me if I would like company and I told him sure. Our conversation became so interesting that we past my destination of the baseball park. Passing my destination played a major role in my life. This was a key moment that would forever change the LORDs plan for my life.

Once I passed the park I found myself staring in the window of a store that had products I had never seen before. A lot had changed in my little town. It had grown in many ways. I found diversity and culture that was not there before. People with new ideas had opened businesses. The store that I became intrigued by was quite different.

In this store were papers with the strangest writings on them. I became very inquisitive. My desire to know more about the items that were for sale consumed me. Egyptian art and statues. I was impressed. I believed that there was wisdom on the shelves of this store. I felt pulled into the store by either a yearning or my own curiosity. Once I entered the store the owner reached out his hand to shake mine. I complied and at first glance I sensed that this owner was wise. I do not know why I believed this to be true, but I did. Something was drawing me to this store. Something was pulling at me. It wanted me to find out more about the wisdom that I was to gain here.

After speaking with the store owner, I was convinced the more that he was wise. It seemed that every question I asked, he replied with wisdom and it brought about a level of understanding that I had not previously had. He even answered many of my long-awaited questions. An opportunity had been afforded to me and I would not miss it. I dared not to be let down again. Since the opportunity had presented itself I would take the chance to ask questions without feeling ridiculed. I knew that this time things would be different. I was standing in a place where people could grow. I could feel it. I was surrounded by wisdom. I was surrounded by books.

The store owner embraced me and my friend as his students. That summer we visited him almost every day. Over time I wanted to be closer to the teacher and his wisdom. I decided to move back to my home town. The presence of peace that was around me was encouraging. As time went on, he taught me about healthy eating and the things of nature. He spoke about meditation and said that he would teach me how to meditate one day. Under his tutelage I studied health and nature along with the history of the African American people.

One day my teacher introduced me to a book called the Quran. He invited me to study it with him. He informed me that studying It and living according to its precepts has made him a better person. Together we read the Quran as well as other Islamic teachings by other authors. As time went on I learned that my instructor had someone in his life whom he considered to be his teacher. He said that he was an inspiration to him and spoke of him as being the master teacher.

While studying Islam I found myself feeling satisfied with my new teachings and no longer concerned with the things of the church. I was learning and getting what I needed to sustain myself spiritually. I was no longer assaulted with unfulfilling teachings from the pulpit.

Through Islamic teachings I was introduced to the true meaning of prayer and its necessity. I understood the reverencing of God. It was during this time in my life that I learned the meaning of worship. To honor Allah was my new way of life. Allah was to be honored and respected above all. Prayer was very important in my new walk to better understanding God. I had never understood prayer as intimacy with God. I was now taking specific times out of my day to please and connect with Allah.

This was a change. Growing up in church, my experience of prayer was that that it was not a big deal. Prayer seemed to be a necessity that hindered the church service from moving on. For this reason it was rushed through so that we could get to the important things of the service. Prayer seemed to be done out of obligation and not love, intimacy or sacrifice.

This was not the case where the teachings of the god Allah was concerned. Yet even in my delight of prayer and submission unto Allah, there began a nagging taking place within my heart. It was strange but suddenly, I became concerned about having two Gods in my life. It was then that my teacher explained to me that I was really serving one God, called by different names due to the difference of languages spoken in other parts of the world.

I was told by my teacher that the God named Allah in the Quran was the same God in the Bible. Satisfied with an answer that was sensible, I was comforted and believed that I had done nothing wrong.

At the point of my unsettled heart being comforted, I was relieved and ready to continue in my studies for educational and spiritual growth in the teachings of Islam. I was free of a gossiping atmosphere and the attitudes of the women in the church. I was now being embraced with wisdom of womanhood and surrendering myself unto Allah. All that I learned was found useful for my daily growth. Surrounded by people who were putting Allah first, loving one another, and doing community work I went on to grow in Allah.

I experienced sisterhood in the Mosque and as far as I could see, we all had a common desire. To be a great example of a servant, wife, and mother. The women were peaceful, and I wanted to be in a place of peaceful women who wanted to learn how to love Allah in a studious, prayerful, and intimate way. For the first time, I felt truly accepted in what I was told was God's house.

CHAPTER 6

MANIPULATED

It was In confusion and frustration that I walked away from the church and eventually began attending mosque. Not long afterwards I decided that it was time for me to take my Salaat. This, I was taught was considered one of the most significant acts of worship a Muslim can perform. I took part in the month of Ramadan and basically everything that a Muslim would do concerning the Quran and life as a believer.

The clothing that I wore totally changed and I found it honorable and respectful to be modest by covering both my body and my hair. I denounced the teachings of Christianity and focused on Islam alone.

There were times when I had a sense of doubt concerning totally forgetting about the church. Each time that this would occur, my doubts were put to rest and I was comforted with the wisdom of the text. It began to be even the more instilled in me that it did not matter that I called God by the name Allah. My teacher went as far as to explain to me that Jesus never spoke English and since it was not the original language it was fine to call God by a different name. He assured me that God was not offended by being called Allah. Again, being comforted, I believed that I would be fine spiritually.

As time went on I learned that my teacher had a teacher whom he adored. He said that this man was an inspiration to him and spoke of him as being a master teacher. Being under his influence it was not long before the teachings of this master teacher became relevant in my life as well. It was not long before the Quran was no longer my main source of spiritual value. Without my understanding of what was happening I was becoming indoctrinated

I was informed by my teacher that the master teacher was moving us away from the teachings of Islam and into another way of life. He said that only things that are dead don't change. I made the decision to leave Islam and follow the advice of my teacher. It was at this point that things began to change in my life and I grew confused. Strange things began to happen to me. I began having paranormal experiences. These encounters were both evil and irrelevant to healthy spiritual growth that I intended on having. These spiritual encounters were not of the LORD. I was experiencing a dark side of spirituality and did not understand how to handle it.

Not knowing what I had gotten myself into I realized that I was in trouble. In my trouble, I decided to stay under the teachings of my teacher since he was the one who had begun me on my journey for Godly wisdom. He was also the only person who understood me spiritually. Besides, I cared for my mentor. He was there for me when I was lost in understanding God. I figured that he would assist me as soon as he knew how.

In the very beginning of these paranormal experiences I was not intellectually able to connect my spiritual troubles being caused by my new way of life. It was not long before I began denying the bible and its teachings all together. It was at this point that the angels of the LORD who had watched over me and guided me from childhood took a back seat to the strange events taking place in my life. Three angels of the LORD stood in a corner to my left and wrote things down concerning me. They did not speak to me, nor did they assist me during my struggle. I did not understand why, so I observed their actions towards me. Gradually I realized that my relationship with the LORD was being severed.

Once this became evident to me I began thinking things through. First, I denounced Christianity and became a Muslim. I studied Islam and then left that to study spiritualism in a new form. I realized that this was the problem. My spiritual life was way out there, and this new move broke my connection with the LORD in a greater way. I began to understand that it was for these reason that the LORD removed his presence from me. He was displeased with what I had become. I was no longer clear concerning that which was right or wrong concerning spirituality.

Wisdom Key:

Many years later I learned from the Holy Spirit that I had no excuse for walking away from the church despite my reasoning. It was my responsibility to seek wisdom and not to stop until I found it. Had I done so, my life would have taken a better turn. Sure, I had been mistreated in the church. It was also true that I was not taught well when I attended church services. Still, according to the Holy Spirit there was no excuse. According to the revelation that I received, I was responsible for my actions. Since I chose these actions, I would have to deal with the consequences of my actions. I was going to have to wait until the LORD decided to show mercy upon me and send me the assistance that I needed.

From this point on in the book, you may find me using the term "the enemy". When doing so I am referring to satan and his demons.

CHAPTER 7

MISLED

Upon accepting this new teaching into my life. I became victimized by demon spirits. They abused me and from time to time they would give me a resting period from their torture. The allowance of this resting period was never due to any sort of compassion I am sure. It was to be used as a form of manipulation at a later date. Their main objective was to pretend to be of help to me. These claimed to be my ancestors and their assistance of getting me out of a trap from time to time came with a price.

When in trouble concerning spiritual matters, they would pretend to come to my aid. They adopted me in. This was to make me believe that I would be safe if I remained with them. I was indebted because there was a price to pay when you were a part of their family. When attempting to remove myself from their bondage I was always met with helpers. These helpers were not actually helpers I learned later. They were a team of demons who pretended to come to my rescue. Their agenda was to place me in a cycle of torment under the authority of several teams of demons.

Once the teaching changed I recognized through conversating with other people the change of mindset. I learned then that I was not the only one who was being negatively affected by this new ideology.

CHAPTER 8

AMID THE OCCULT

While going through some tough times in my marriage my teacher attempted to assist us. His remedy was for me to meditate. He said it would help me to deal with the stress that I was under. He gave me the instructions and showed me the chart that displayed essential oils needed for clarity and relaxation.

I had never heard of this relaxation technique, so I did some research at the health food store and found a book on meditation as well as the essential oils I should use. Nothing that I read seemed alarming. I concluded that this meditation would be safe.

After doing my research I set some time aside to meditate and heal from my troubles. I followed exact instructions and took some deep breaths but felt nothing new. Frustrated at my failed attempt at meditation I took a hot bath and prepared myself for bed.

Once I became comfortable and almost asleep a buzzing began to take place in my mouth. It felt as though there were bee's moving around very fast. My body began to shake and not long afterwards my spirit sat up and left my physical body. I recall my spirit lifting out of my physical body in the position of one who is sitting up in the bed. It then turned to the right, allowing my feet to hang over the bed and then it stood up and out of my body.

My spirit then walked out of my room and began walking through the walls of the house. Eventually my spirit left the house and began traveling throughout the atmosphere. This activity did not happen on this occasion only. Almost every evening my spirit was taken through this process. I found my spirit leaving my physical body to float through the walls and ceilings until it reached a way of getting out into the atmosphere and soaring from one place to another.

Over time, I encountered many different spiritual beings on many different levels. Each had their own purpose in my life. They were distinguished in appearance and at times claimed to be my family. They stated that they had been looking for me and that they wanted to help me. They said how glad they were that they found me. They appeared to be glad but for what reason, I did not know at the time. I later learned the reason. They wanted to take me far away from the LORD.

They spoke different languages, which I only understood while I was in their plane of existence. Some spoke to me telepathically. These spiritual beings were very intellectual. They were wise. They had the ability to look at me with a piercing stare that made me feel as though they were looking directly through me. They looked at me as though they were reading a book. This placed fear in me concerning trying to report them to someone. Trying to find someone to cause them to leave me alone. Because of this fear I stayed in silence concerning many of my spiritual abuses.

Daily they would visit me. They appeared to want to replace the Holy Spirit and the angels of the LORD in my life. In the beginning and several times when necessary they treated me like family. This was done so I would no longer missed the Holy Spirit and the LORDs angels as much as I did before. I must add that this level of family love and connection was on a different level than what I had previously experienced with the LORD and the spiritual impact that it had upon my life was different as well.

There came a time when these dark spiritual beings started forcing me out of my body and my home without my meditating. They had access to me and caused this removal at their own will. These demonic spiritual beings had the ability to call my spirit out of my body from a distance. They were also able to pull on my spirit from a distance without saying a word to me. There were times my spirit would leave on its own because it was so accustomed to not remaining still when I was in a position of quiet and rest. So, once I would lay down to rest, my spirit felt the need to leave as if it were not tired and had plans of its own. It was terrible not having control over the actions of my own body.

The vortexes that I found myself being forcefully pulled into while I was in the spirit realm were deep and dark. So dark that I cannot explain their color because it does not exist in this earth. I had to work my way through these vortexes and the different levels of darkness. It was difficult to find my way back to my body. I also met spirit beings in the atmosphere while I was attempting to find my way back to my body. There were some cases where the spiritual beings that I had met were set in place to manipulate and befriend me by pretending to want to help me to get back into my body.

At times like these, I experienced a fear that I had never known before. It was a different level of fear because I was in an unknown place. Things that used to be simple, like thinking, had to be done strategically. I had to concentrate on the process of thinking. There were times when I would find my way back to my body all by myself, but then I did not know how to get inside. I would find myself elevated within my bedroom ceiling, encouraging my spirit to get back in, but it would not. My heart would pound in the physical realm while lying in my body. At times like these I panicked.

Demonic spiritual beings took advantage of this and pretended to rescue me. They attempted to befriend me. They would come and soar with me. They would look at my body along with me, waiting and watching. One day, a female spiritual being came by. She looked at my body with me, and said, "So you cannot get back in? Let me help you." When she helped me, I was obligated to her for a season. This was also the case with other spiritual beings. I rarely received any assistance out of pure generosity. You see, I could not stop leaving my body on my own, and these demonic spirits knew this. They used it to their advantage to build a trusting relationship so I would depend upon them as I depended on the LORD when I was in right relationship with him.

In each area of suffering, I found that there were lessons I needed to learn. This is what I learned. Meditation is a good thing, but it can be dangerous if done incorrectly and with the wrong intentions. Someone invited me to get away from the stresses of the world by meditating, which seemed simple, but I should have done more research. I should have asked more questions. But I trusted the individual who informed me about those deep-breathing techniques. I thought those techniques were not a bad thing because I had seen charts describing them in the health food store. My logic was wrong.

When I thought that I was praying or meditating, I was actually doing a technique that would open my chakras. That was dangerous for me. I had been very sensitive to the spirit realm since my youth, so it only took one exercise of deep breathing exercises for it to be effective. I did not believe that I had even performed the meditation correctly because after finishing the technique my emotions did not change. I remained under an immense amount of stress.

Over time I began reaching extremely high levels of vibration. This vibration is necessary for a person to transform into the spirit realm. A person's spirit cannot soar in the atmosphere without reaching the necessary level of vibration to come out of the physical body. This is the reason for the vibration. Today I understand that my actions were preparing my body for astral projection. These meditation exercises were the key.

Astral projection was the way demons gained access to my physical and spiritual body. Once they found me to be a vessel that they could connect with they did with me as they pleased. They placed me under a trance so that they could use my body as a vessel to accomplish their goals.

Ungodly spirit beings would come for me through my windows and through my walls, seeking to take me with them. My body responded to them naturally when they called my spirit out. After a while the spirit beings that pretended to be my family became more forceful and aggressive with me. They began to probe and prick me. They conducted what seemed to be tests on me.

I recall being taken away with them when they deposited some things into my spirit. At this point they had sexual intercourse with me by lowering their vibration to come into a more natural physical body.

Things in my life were bad spiritually. Honestly, I had no idea that things could get any worse, but they did.

One evening after my husband and I put the children to bed, I went to take a shower. While taking my shower, I heard the doorknob turning so I told my husband to come in, but he never responded to me.

Peeking my head out of the shower when I heard the door knob turning I yelled for my husband to come in. Finally, he yelled back from wherever he was and asked me why I was I calling him. I said, "Someone keeps turning the doorknob, and I thought it was you. I thought you needed to come in." He said he did not and then continued what he'd been doing.

The doorknob turned again. This time, it was forceful and loud. Concerned, I pulled back the shower curtain to see what was going on. What I witnessed scared me terribly. I saw the door knob turning and then a very dark spirit walk through the bathroom door and stepped into the shower with me. Uncontrollably I began to scream. Hysterical, I almost fell while in the shower. My husband ran into the bathroom and started looking around. He asked me what was wrong, but I could not speak at the time because I could not stop screaming and jumping.

Grabbing me out of the shower, my husband took me into the living room. He gathered some frankincense oil and attempted to clean the atmosphere of our home. He was attempting to bring about peace and relaxation for me. He placed it upon my forehead and then burned the rest of it in our home. He was angry but could do very little. What he was able to do was try and comfort me from my fear. He started praying for my safety. Unknowingly he and I were praying to the same demons that attacked me. Therefore, our prayers were not effective.

Over time things became more hectic. I began being attacked by demon spirits randomly. This horrific experience would happen at any given time. Whether my husband and I were going for a ride in the car, having a casual conversation or just hanging out. Frustration troubled us but there was nothing that we could do but pray and wait for this season of trouble to end.

Things went from bad to worse. My teacher had no explanation for my experiences. He expressed that he no longer had answers for me. I was then left to fend for myself. It was not long before the demons that were attacking me took me with them to show me an event that would take place. I witnessed my teacher dying. The next day I went to his store and told him that I saw him while I was traveling. I told him what he was doing when I saw him. He confirmed that I was correct about his activity during that time. He looked at me and said you look like you want to say more. He said, why do you look sad. I thought about it and then figured that I did not want to speak negatively to such an honorable man in my sight. So, I told him that I did not have anything else to say concerning what I witnessed. I did not feel that I should tell him that I witnessed him dying because I did not want to believe that It would happen. My teacher asked me if I had something else that I wanted to tell him. I replied by telling him no. a few weeks later I heard the news that he had died. I was heartbroken.

KEY POINT. There is something interesting about how people can introduce you to something, but they have no idea how it might affect you. In the end, they are unable to help you. They leave you all alone to fend for yourself.

when all of this began taking place in my life, my teacher and I were studying ancient history. When he was no longer able to assist me, a new spiritual door opened for me. It was supposed to be meant to release me from my bondage in the spiritual realm. For a while this worked. Ancestral worship helped me because I was lost in the spirit realm and unable to get free. I was told that I needed to call upon my ancestors to escape from the dark spiritual forces (demons) that were haunting and tormenting me. This was the answer that I found helpful at the time.

After dabbling in this for a season, I recognized that I was in danger.

KEY POINT:
I learned that it's a good thing to let the dead remain dead. It is okay to show respect for one's elders or ancestors by keeping a picture of them or studying your history. But that is as far as we should take things. We should never invoke them for assistance no matter what we are going through. Ancestral worship is dangerous and is nothing that a child of God should entertain. It opened and channeled me into places that were not spiritually healthy. If you or anyone you know is experiencing anything like this, my advice is to let the dead remain dead until they are raised up on Judgment Day. I want to take the time to remind you that ancestral worship can be done without one even understanding what they are doing. I have seen instances where people have done simple meditation exercises and have found themselves locked into a spiritual war zone.

CHAPTER 9

ANOTHER LEVEL

Spiritually, I was in a place that I had never known existed. It appears each day I had become a different person. I began to gain insight on things I had never known, read about, or studied. I had a new type of self-knowledge. Eventually I learned that information was being deposited into my mind by wicked spiritual beings.

These spirits had lodged themselves within my body and were feeding me knowledge from their realm of existence. They pretended to embrace me in a healthy spiritual manner. They called me family and ordained me as their spiritual daughter. What I learned eventually was that these beings hated the LORD. The LORD loved me, and they wanted to hurt him by using me as their tool or protégé.

They wanted to use me to accomplish their mission on Earth. They wanted to connect with me spiritually as long-lost ancestral parents. These dark spirits wanted me to curse the name of the LORD. They came into my spirit and attempted to use me to do wrong in the eyes of the LORD.

Eventually, I realized that these beings did not love me. Something awakened inside of me one day, and I remembered again. I was no longer confused. I no longer feared what these demonic forces would do to me if I told someone what they were doing to me. I just knew that I had a family that loved me. I began to gain consciousness about who I was. I remembered the angels of the LORD. I recollected how they used to rescue me and be there for me as the LORD had appointed them to do. I just wanted to be back with the Holy Spirit again like I was when I was in my youth, before I met the spiritual teacher at the store that summer afternoon.

Now that I knew that I wanted my LORD there before me stood an obstacle. I did not know how to go about it. I did not know how to get back to my Lord Jesus, who I knew loved me. I wanted to end this entire place of confusion in my life. The evil spirits knew that I wanted to go back home because they were connected to me. That is when the threats began on a higher level of torment.

These demonic spiritual beings threatened me by telling me that they could see and hear everything that I did. I believed them because they had already proved it. When I attempted to cry out for the Holy Spirit to help me, he did not come. This was discouraging, and I thought that I would anger the demonic spirits by calling the Holy Spirit to come help me so I stopped.

My spirit was very dark by now and I had lost even more control over my life than I had before. Over time within my torment I figured that the LORD no longer wanted me. I did the only thing that I knew how to do, and that was to find my own way around the spirit realm. I had to fight for my peace. I stepped up my worship and escalated my idolatry. I started using candles during my meditations. I was desperate and tried to do whatever I could to be released from this spiritual dark plane of existence. I attempted to build some spiritual strength of my own. I just wanted to survive. I was in survival mode. I needed an escape route. I figured that it was best to try to get along with the dark spiritual forces, since I could not defeat them.

I was a slave to them. I was in the deepest form of spiritual darkness that that a person could be. When my husband could not protect me from these beings, I decided it was best to just get along with them until I could find a way out. This still did not work, but it was worth a try.

KEY POINT: Not all meditation is good and acceptable in the eyes of our LORD. Satan will come in a form that you trust to offer you his deceit. Do a lot of research before trying new relaxation and meditation techniques. It could take you down an awful path of spiritual wreckage. Meditation practices come in many different forms. Some people call them cleansing breaths. Some will attempt to teach you how to breathe into an area where there is pain and frustration, claiming that you will be healed. Be prayerful as well as wise. Dig deep before you begin any new form of spiritual relaxing techniques.

Your rescuer may come bringing you a promise of gladness by teaching you to focus on the area of the body that is diseased or damaged. Over time while I was in my state of bondage, I was taught to vibrate my vocal cord and to locate the chakra in my body. I was told to activate the center solar plexus. I was taught to visualize the color of the chakras to light them up. For a while, I had a blast. I was learning and experiencing new things. I was learning how to meditate to calm my nerves and relax through stressful situations. It was all a lie. But by the time that I found that out, it was too late. I was tricked by an agent of Satan, who came to me in the form of a helper. This helper came to me bearing wisdom. Wisdom that I could not afford to keep.

It is a sad fact that the average person who comes to your aid, assisting you in spiritual understanding means well. They do not know that they are being used as agents of the devil to take you off the righteous path that the LORD has set you on. They are simply doing what they think is best, helping someone in need.

Unfortunately, their assistance can lead to your destruction and possibly your death.

Allow me to give you an example of the craftiness of these demons. One morning I got up to fix breakfast. It was 4:30 a.m. I took a shower and then put a pot of water on the stove, so I could make some oatmeal for the children. I went back to my bedroom and sat on the edge of my bed waiting for the water to boil and planning my day.

I began to feel mist in my room and saw some dark spiritual beings standing there. Suddenly I felt a pulling on my spirit. It felt like suction, like a very strong vacuum was pulling on me. The dark spirit beings had what looked like fans spinning in their stomach. That which looked like fans in their stomach then began pulling me towards them. It was like the suction that takes place when a person places their hand close to the attachment of a vacuum, except it was a lot more uncomfortable. The suction was extremely strong and as it was taking place the dark spirit beings came closer. They pulled on my spirit a little harder than they had the first time. I was totally frightened. I begged and pleaded with them. "Please don't take me," I said. "My stove, my kids. Please don't take me." They continued to pull on my spirit despite my pleading cries.

While I was being pulled in the spirit realm I had very little voice for the fight because my spirit was being separated. One last tug was done, and I found myself on my way into outer darkness once again. I was no longer in my physical body. Once again, I was vulnerable and at their mercy.

When I was taken, my family was still asleep. I did not know how long they would keep me this time and it frightened me. These spirit beings placed me in this tub like thing that had fluid inside of it. They transported their fluids inside of me and kept me there with them for a time. While with them, I could not comprehend time but felt as though I was there for a very long time.

They bathed me in this slimy fluid, and then took me to a spirit being that was at the very top of a place indoors, and he had sex with me. The women spirits prepared me and took me to this ugly spirit and he did things that were unexplainable to my spirit. The next thing that I remembered was that the spirits took me back home.

When I came back and was adjusted into my physical body, I ran into the kitchen to check the water in the pot. It had almost boiled out. Smoke was steaming from the scorched pot. I was angry. These beings were out of control. They were aggressive and selfish. I was so tired of this constant craziness in my life. I wanted to be normal again. I just wanted to find someone who could defeat these demons. The spiritual beings that continued to torment me were like abusers. They would threaten me with harm. They seemed to always make good on their promises and they had no remorse.

The difficult thing about being attacked in the spiritual realm is that there are no police that can be called to rescue you. If this was happening to me in the natural realm, I would have a law that could be used to protect me but in the spiritual realm I had no one and I was all alone.

I could not go to the church with my trouble since I had not been successful being understood in the past. Since I could not get assistance in understanding my supernatural experiences in the past, I could just forget about telling someone in the church about the type of demonic situations that I was going through.

That's when I decided to pray for myself again. This really didn't help me much because I came to realize that I was praying to another set of ancestors, which I found out were demons. I was praying to them to help me get away from the spiritual beings that were hurting me. Over time I learned that they were all demons. Naturally my prayers did not work. When it was all said and done, I was praying to the same demons that were hurting me except they were from a different troop.

I can only imagine how this makes no sense to you but at the time this was all that I knew. Over time it felt as though my mind had not only been deceived but sucked dry like a milkshake through a straw. By this time, all I really knew was my abuser. I had been in relationship with these beings and away from The Great I Am for eleven years by this time. That was eleven years of torture with small breaks of peace from time to time.

KEY POINT: If you are in this type of situation, you can get out simply by calling on the name of the Lord Jesus. Repent from your sins, and ask for forgiveness. Don't be ashamed to ask a minister of the gospel whom you trust for help. You don't have to stay stuck for years like I did. I didn't know any better or have anyone to teach me right from wrong where spiritual things are concerned. I was also in bondage under the spirit of confusion. Under this form of bondage, I had no understanding of how to get back to the LORD.

Although I had sinned against the LORD attempting to find him in a different religion and by calling him by another name, he wanted to help me. I was trapped and unable to be liberated until I learned that it was the LORD who could help me. He helped me through Jesus. Jesus was a living sacrifice for the sins of all of mankind. Power was given to us because of that sacrifice. When we call upon Jesus, we can be delivered out of the hands of the enemy. Once you get into these practices, it will take the blood of Jesus's sacrifice to get you out.

The power of the Holy Spirit will keep you safe. During my bondage, I didn't know enough to call upon the name of the Lord Jesus. I never learned about salvation or the blood sacrifice of Jesus. My help was limited. I came up in a town where preachers yelled sermons filled with nothing. It was all about being loud and showboating. Today I have been exposed to great teaching ministries.

People in this generation seem to want more. They want answers and wisdom. They want explanations for who, what, where, when and why? If they do not receive these answers they seek to find them somewhere else. When I was growing up as a teen I was not aware of any internet. The options that people have today were not available to me.

CHAPTER 10

BRICK CHURCH

My family and I moved to new town which we all loved. Right around the corner from where we lived was a brick church. Each time I drove past this church I felt as though there was a connection being made. This made very little sense to me since I was not interested in attending any churches at all.

In my time of living in this town there were many churches, but none tugged at me in a way that made me wonder. There seemed to be something lingering around this building, but I did not understand what it was.

Whenever I drove past the church, my eyes would always lock onto it. I could not understand why I had this intense desire to connect with this church. Way deep down in my insides was a feeling that I had never experienced before. Something was different. Something was calling me to this brick church.

CHAPTER 11

HOLY SPIRIT RESCUE

Still stuck in this evil tormenting state of being due to the mistake that I had made as a teenager, I was exhausted. In my exhaustion, I continued to go on with my daily routine as best as I could. Things began to change within the teachings of the master teacher. He was now teaching that his followers were to be identified as the Nuwaubian Nation of Moors.

As an organization there were many gatherings. The idea was that everyone was family and people were encouraged to do things as a family. For a season, one evening a week was set aside for family discussions. In the beginning the gatherings were somewhat enjoyable. Food, fun, laughter and the joining together of one another for chats. Not long after things began to change.

The master teacher began making statements that in my opinion were unnecessary. He said that Jesus was not who the bible recorded him to be. He began cursing the name of Jesus regularly and went as far as to make very negative statements about him while calling him names.

He said that Jesus was a homosexual and things of that nature. He said that students had to prove they had not been brainwashed into believing that they would go to hell if they cursed the name and person of Jesus. They behaved accordingly. If a person hesitated to curse the name of Jesus or say rude things about Jesus, they were considered to have fear instilled within them. They were looked at as though they had fear of the Bible, its threats, and promised condemnations.

This made no sense to me because if we did not believe in Jesus and if he had no significance, why did we mention him? I voiced my concerns with some whom I considered sisters and we talked about it.

One evening the master teacher said some horrible things about Jesus and all that he stood for. He went on a tangent. He went overboard stating that he had proof of the homosexual acts of Jesus. His comments were disgusting.

After a while the master teacher's voice became dim to my ears. I could see his mouth moving but could not hear the words that he spoke. It was then that I noticed him looking at me differently. It was as if he could tell that something was happening to me. It was then that his eyes changed. His eyes began to shine in a way that I have only seen in an individual who is demonically possessed by Beelzebub.

Suddenly I heard a new sound. My hearing was improving but now it was connected to a different spiritual being. While I listened to this new voice, the master teacher looked on, and for what seemed like a minute he stopped teaching all together. Then I heard words within my heart at first. These words were spoken softly and then audibly.

All at once I reviewed all that I had learned from my mentor, the one who introduced me to this master teacher. This voice spoke truth to me, and it made my heart glad. Whenever the master teacher spoke, this new spiritual being would interrupt my mind and eardrums and speak the truth into my heart.

I seemed to be waking up to the truth. I could now recognize the lie that had been inserted into my mind concerning Jesus. The master teacher continued teaching and began making more statements regarding Jesus, but when he did the voice of the spirit being would answer the statement for me using biblical scripture. Things started to make sense to me. It was as though a light had been turned on in my mind.

At the end of the night my attitude and connection to the leader and his mission had changed. I wanted out! While my mind was being reconditioned, I received an open vision of one of those old-fashioned skeleton keys. That night the unlocking of my mind began and there was a cleansing taking place within my mind and heart.

Once my mind was totally unlocked, the spirit being introduced himself to me as the Holy Spirit. "I have come to release you from this bondage," the Holy Spirit said to me. "I have come to help you in your desperate time of need," he said, softly into my heart. I began shaking my head with amazement and thought to myself, *You couldn't have come at a better time.* Then I had to recant. I took a few deep breaths and said to myself, *Yes, you could have.*

My mind had been tormented and I had a lot of memory loss due to the continual astral travel and meeting of different spiritual beings. I had been tricked by so many spirits, and I was still confused. Torment had changed my mindset. Astral projection held me captive, removing my spirit from my body by force for over an eleven year period.

I needed healing in my mind. Every spiritual being that connected to me lied concerning who I was to them. Due to the manipulation that I had experienced during this time of being away from the one true God, I needed to be positive that this spirit whom I was now conversing with was truly the Holy Spirit that I had known in my youth. I needed to test the motives of this spiritual being. I had been tricked so many times before that I was going to take my time and examine this connection. I had to figure out if this spirit being was really who he said that he was.

I felt at peace with him, but I had felt at peace with others in the past, that is, until they revealed their identities and agendas for my life. Even though he told me who he was, I still had to gain a trusting relationship with him because of the many others who had come into my life.

I had to try this one out first before I gave into him and allowed a trusting relationship to be formed. I must say that from the very beginning, I felt different about this one. This spirit being came with mental healing and biblical truth. This spirit being defended Jesus Christ and his ministry on the earth.

He spoke well of Jesus and taught me about the Bible. Our relationship was not just a series of spiritual experiences. It was healthy Bible teaching and lessons about holiness. He taught me the Word of God. This was the difference between him and the others I had encountered over the eleven-year period. I began to believe that I could let go of my fear and allow this spiritual being to rescue me as he said that he had come to do. I felt that I could trust him.

Both verbally and within my heart, I gave the LORD glory in a huge way. It was time that I become released from spiritual bondage. The LORD sent the Holy Spirit to remove me from the world of the occult. It was time for me to learn the biblical truth about Jesus and not just rely on experiences and encounters. It was time for me to know why Jesus had been sent into the world. The Holy Spirit was the one who could teach me. "It is time to bring you back home to us, your true family," the Holy Spirit said to me.

Each day, the Holy Spirit taught me. We became great friends all over again. It was wonderful to be reacquainted with him. It was great to be in a right relationship with The Great I Am and to be with my real spiritual family. As my private classes with the Holy Spirit went on, I learned that Jesus was not who I'd been told he was. He was not insignificant. He was necessary and important to the world and to mankind.

The Holy Spirit allowed me to see images in the spirit realm; the skeleton key that unlocked my mind now unlocked spiritual chains from around my head. The Holy Spirit understood my learning style, and I believe that's why he showed me images of what had taken place in my life over the years. I already knew about the side effects, but the Holy Spirit wanted me to see the root cause of my trouble. As this was happening, I woke up from the terrible nightmare I had been in for more than eleven years.

The Holy Spirit comforted me. He gave me insight into all the lies that had been fed to me. At first, I was amazed; I then I felt foolish. I thought to myself, *How could I have believed these things?* I now understood what it meant to be a master teacher. I believed those lies because he was good at persuading the people who followed him into bondage and controlling their thoughts and minds. He was a master at manipulating both people and situations. Although I was frustrated about all that had happened, I knew that everything would be okay. I knew this because the Holy Spirit was back in my life.

CHAPTER 12

REACQUAINTING

Once I left the cult compound and gained a trusting relationship with the Holy Spirit, he asked me to do something for him. "I want you to find a church that will teach you about the biblical Jesus," the Holy Spirit said to me. This made sense because I had already known and experienced Jesus spiritually but not biblically.

I heard the testimonies of the ministers. I heard what they had to say about life and their version of what Christianity meant to them. In the end, it was just words and personal stories but nothing biblical. What was being shared with my young mind from the pulpit was not pure biblical teaching but paraphrasing and personal stories. This was not as effective and did nothing for my spiritual growth in the LORD.

Here I have the Holy Spirit explaining to me his desire for me to leave my past and move forward. I was to seek understanding concerning the biblical Jesus. I began on this journey as a teenager. My mind had been conditioned and I had many great relationships with people who were still a part of the cult. Although I was determined to be obedient to the Holy Spirit, I struggled letting go of the emotional ties that had been formed over the years. The Holy Spirit was very caring and could see that I was hurting in this area. He then began to explain to me in a loving and caring way that these relationships that I had formed were not healthy. He gave me not only strength to leave them but also the wisdom to understand why they were detrimental to my future growth with the LORD.

The Holy Spirit revealed the God of the bible to me and gave me lots of love. He knew how broken and tormented I had been during my bondage, and he renewed my strength and my hope. I considered finding a church where I could learn about Jesus Christ properly. The only thing holding me back was my sorrowful past experiences. I had many doubts concerning the church. After my many teachings of deep revelation and knowledge, I began to question if what I were to learn in church would be enough for me. Over the years I had been accustomed to a lot of teaching from many books. Now I was expected to learn from one book alone.

My mind had been conditioned to seek a certain type of teaching and going back to the biblical teaching of my childhood was discouraging. I wondered if it would be alright with the Holy Spirit if I just left the occult, all its practices, and lived a normal life. I wondered if he would not mind if I left the matter of church all together and just enjoyed him and my spiritual family of my youth.

As my thoughts began to form, the Holy Spirit heard them and immediately began to comfort my uneasy heart. He explained to me that he was very sure that I would one day find joy in the LORDs church. It was then that my mind was at peace. I decided to give church another try.

My love relationship with the Holy Spirit was growing daily. Within the time of him coming to the cult campground, awakening me from my spiritual slumber and rescuing me, he had done so much. My love for him had grown so deep that I wanted to give something back to him. He was my friend and I did not want our relationship to be one sided. I did not want him to be the only one giving and sacrificing in our relationship. It was true love that we shared, and I needed to do my part and be obedient to the things that he asked of me.

The Holy Spirit wanted to help me get back on the right track with the Father. I believed him and made some steps to show my dedication to our new life and journey together. Even in all my good intentions, I found myself reluctant to get out there and find a church where I could learn of the biblical Jesus, as he had previously requested. With my mouth, I declared to the Holy Spirit that I would find a church. I even planned to do it in my mind, but I procrastinated. The Holy Spirit noticed this and allowed my health to be touched. My procrastination came to an end when I noticed that sickness began to touch my mind and body.

My mind felt as though it was being sucked dry. Because of this I was unable to process my thoughts properly. Suddenly my flowing bank account and decent employment was gone, and my finances began to dwindle away. My home began being infested with bugs and the children and I would watch them streaming down the walls and in the television. We all got together going from room to room killing the bugs. It made no sense to me because we went from having no bugs to being infested in one day. Services for my home were being disconnected and we no longer had water service due to nonpayment. I came under an extreme amount of stress.

In my despair, the Holy Spirit again suggested that I go to church to learn of the biblical Jesus Christ. I said that I would and this time I meant it. I totally surrendered to his will. I told him I would seek out a church but that I needed his help.

I remained distressed despite my agreement to find a church. When a coworker of mine noticed my demeanor, she took me to the side and revealed that she had just accepted Jesus as her Lord and savior. She asked me to come into the cooler with her so that we could pray.

She said she believed that if I prayed with her, my situation would change for the better. With a convincing look upon her face she stated that she was no preacher but that she had just got saved and believed that Jesus could help me with my problem. Even at her sincere request I hesitated. Again, she asked me to pray with her. I took some time to think about it. I was not secure in my thinking about prayer being what I needed.

My coworker noticed my hesitation but was bold in her desire to help me get out of my dilemma. It was then that she pushed the issue even more. I was still unsure about the effects of prayer but to keep her from holding me hostage in the cold freezer and to keep her from bothering me again, I agreed. Due to my distraction, I am not sure what was said during the prayer. Once it was over I livened up. She let go of my hands and I proceeded in my worries.

I did not get away easily. Shortly after the prayer the Holy Spirit reminded me that I'd promised to find a church to settle in and learn of Jesus. Exhausted with fighting with him, I decided to seek out a church after work. Driving around town, I noticed that every church that I approached was closed. With one hand on the steering wheel and the other on my forehead, I thought, *The doors of the church are always supposed to be open, aren't they?*

Eventually I found a church in the town. It was on top of a hill. The parking lot was empty, so I assumed that they were closed. Then as I began to circle around the parking lot to leave, I noticed a sign that was posted on the church door. Curious, I got of my car to take a closer look at the sign. In bold letters, the sign stated that a church service would begin at 7:00 p.m. Looking at the time I realized that it would be only a few hours until service began so I decided to sit in my car and wait.

It was important that I kept my word to the Holy Spirit this time. It was important to me that I did not choose to procrastinate. Eventually a car drove up and a tall man got out. I hurried over to him and nervously expressed that I was in desperate need of help. Speaking in a soft whisper I said "I think that I may be a sinner."

The man looked at me strangely. With a concerned tone of voice he asked me to come into his office so we could talk. Nervous I walked into the church with him. It had been a while since I had stepped foot into a church and I did not want to deal with the judgmental mindset that received in my youth. Once we sat down I began explaining why I believed I might be a sinner. I told him that I used to be a part of a cult that was in town. I explained my confusion concerning sin.

Noticing how serious I was, his look of concern changed. He realized that I truly needed help. He excused himself from the room, and when he came back he was accompanied by another man who introduced himself as a pastor. Once the pastor was settled in his chair I was asked to repeat what I said. I repeated myself by stating that I thought that I may be a sinner.

The pastor burst out laughing. Once he finished chuckling, he said that if I had not received Jesus as my Lord and savior then I was a sinner indeed. He told me I was living a life of sin. Once I heard those words come out of his mouth I told him about all the things that I did not do. I did not drink. I did not smoke. He looked at me as if he was not impressed so I told him about all the other bad things I did not do.

Still unconvinced, the pastor replied that only receiving Christ Jesus as my personal savior would make things right between me and God. He handed me a Bible, asked me to read it. The pastor then invited me to come back to the church the following Sunday. The two men prayed with me and then I left.

I had now done what the Holy Spirit asked me to do. *I should feel better in just a few minutes*, I thought as I walked to my car. Before I left Christianity, the LORD seemed to answer my hearts cry expeditiously. Naturally, after obeying the Holy Spirit, I was expecting immediate results. I had done my part and was now waiting on the Holy Spirit to remove the burdens and stress from my life.

As I sat and waited, nothing happened! I could not believe it. I was still under an enormous amount of stress and anxiety. My life remained a mess and I worried about how long it would take before I saw a change. I felt awful about my life but great about finally finding a church.

My family and I went to the church the following Sunday. I was hopeful as I witnessed the service begin. I hoped that my family could grow properly in the LORD. I smiled with gladness, but my gladness did not last. I was not able to benefit from the preaching due to the deep southern accent and teaching style.

I was reminded of my childhood experience of sitting in church and not learning. Over time I struggled with my decision to stay at that ministry. Even through my struggle, I was determined to give it a few more weeks before giving up. Obedience to the Holy Spirit kept me there longer than I wanted to stay.

While sitting in church both my heart and mind played tug of war. It was then that I was reminded of the brick church that continued to catch my eye. Frustrated with this process, I decided to leave the church on the hill and go back to being taught by the Holy Spirit. I was accustomed to his teaching style and I enjoyed it. He understood my process of thinking and I saw progress with each lesson

CHAPTER 13

THE COURTEOUS CLERK

It was a beautiful day in Eatonton, Georgia. The Nuwaubian's were holding their annual family picnic. No longer being affiliated I did not go. Even so my emotions were a little unstable due to the memories. The wonderful Holy Spirit had not yet delivered me from the images and experiences that had oppressed me for so long.

It was best that I kept myself busy, so I decided to spend some time in town that afternoon. At the end of my day went to a beautification store. The clerk recognized me as a member and asked if I were going to the picnic? I replied informing her that I was no longer a part of the Nuwaubians. She looked puzzled but did not go into it any further.

She then asked me why I wore so much black. I had no idea why I wore so much black. It all began when the master teacher made an announcement that we were to wear black. I did not understand why he wanted us to wear black. He gave his reasons such as black is a color of authority to the fact that Jews wore black. When he finished explaining his logic it made sense. Therefore, most Nuwaubians followed his logic.

Spiritually the wearing of black was doing something deeper on the inside of me. In the beginning I was not happy wearing black every day. It gave me a dull feeling that led to a depressed state of mind in a settle way. As with time, I adjusted and looked at my clothing as nothing personal but something that I needed to cover myself with. It was easier to deal with.

This conversation gave me a wakeup call concerning the image that I had portrayed for a season of my life. It was not recognizable to me because I liked helping people and had a caring heart. Even though I had reacquainted myself with the Holy Spirit and change was taking place within me, parts of my past still lingered. Our conversation was a key to my understanding that I still had a lot of work to do with the Holy Spirit before I would be made whole.

While chatting with the clerk she showed me some different shades of lipstick to try. I felt that the Holy Spirit was giving me time to warm up to her enough to share my situation with her. I shared with her that I had left the cult and was trying to get my life together and on the correct path with the LORD. She looked concerned and willing to assist me. She told me that there was a prophet down the street and that I should visit his church.

She said that if anyone can help me to get my life together he could. It was at this point that my husband rushed me to the door. In a hurry I asked the clerk where this prophet was, and she wrote down the directions to the church. I thanked the woman and she gathered up my things including the brown earth tone lipstick that I had decided to try.

I wondered if I would take her advice concerning this church. I talked to my husband to see what he thought. He said that he was not sure and that we should leave it alone for the time being.

The following week my husband told me about something he'd noticed at his place of employment. Daily the supervisor gathered his men together for prayer before they clocked in. This behavior intrigued my husband. His dedication made an obvious impression on him because he became curious about the supervisor's motive and daily prayer ritual.

I could see that the Holy Spirit was working on my husband's heart as well. Soon after my husband's supervisor invited him to be a guest at his church.

He was not going to fall for this religious mumbo jumbo. I believed him and figured that he would not accept the man's invitation. Then my husband's mental wheels began to turn. His curiosity got the best of him. He needed to find something wrong with this man's faith and wanted to investigate his church for himself. It was then that I knew our family would be visiting his supervisor's church.

My thoughts were correct. My husband decided to investigate this man's faith in his God. Although my husband said he did not believe in the God of the church, deep down I knew that he wanted to. I believe that the prayers of his family had reached God. His mother's wishes for her son's salvation had a lot to do with what was about to take place. My husband was considering this invitation.

Once my husband came to me with the final decision of going to church, I jumped at the opportunity. Who knew when it would come again. Between the woman at the beauty supply store talking to me and his supervisor inviting him to church I could see the Holy Spirit working. Now we knew that we were going to church, but where. Would we go there the prophet was or would we accept my husband's supervisor's invitation.

The time came for us to attend church. It was a new day for us. I was extremely excited to see what would happen for us as a family. We gathered the directions to the church and headed out the door. As I sat in the passenger seat and read off the directions to my husband I noticed something strange. The directions that I read off were like the ones that the beauty supply clerk had given me. It wasn't long before I realized that the directions were the same.

When my husband pulled up to the church I realized that it was the same brick church that had caught my eye every time I drove by. We all sat in the car for a while as my husband and I began to process this next move in our life. We explained to the children where we were going and that they were to behave themselves. I was nervous but eventually we all got out of the car and walked toward the front door. Once I stepped inside something happened to me from within. There was something familiar about this place. I did not understand, there should not have been anything familiar about the church because I had never been there before.

Once inside I realized what was familiar. It was the presence of my friend the Holy Spirit. I gathered my thoughts and continued to walk further into the church. In the foyer before I walked through the doors leading into the sanctuary I heard an audible voice say, "Take off your shoes, you are on holy ground."

The voice was louder and more distinguished than the voice of the Holy Spirit. Then a quickening took place within my spirit, and I recognized the voice of my old friend and Father, the LORD. I had been away for a very long time, but I still knew that voice. There was no other voice like it. I smiled and continued to walk through the sanctuary doors.

I listened keenly while the sermon was being preached. Wow! There was something different about the manner of this preaching. He taught a message about holiness, righteousness, and obedience. There was a power upon and inside him that I'd only recognized when with the Holy Spirit. A strictness came forth in his preaching. He had a concern for people.

He was kind and friendly, yet he meant business. I had not witnessed this type of congregational care while growing up in church. My experience was that ministers were both rude and careless. My childhood experience was that of ministers who did not seem to care about the people in the church or the God that they claimed to serve.

While the apostle preached from the pulpit, the lovely Holy Spirit allowed me to see both him and the situation in the spirit realm. What was revealed to me was that he was as a statue that had water pouring fourth from its mouth. While viewing this revelation, I listened closely. The atmosphere in this church was beautiful. I felt as if I were being submerged into the LORDs peace. This was a gift to me from the LORD. He knew that I needed to be in a place like this. I took a lot into my spirit that day. My spirit had been so dry and thirsty. I had been in a desert of my own for so many years.

I was receptive to the atmosphere and teaching and then the devil tried to manipulate my mind causing me to feel skeptical of the apostle. The Holy Spirit blessed my mind with peace so that I would remain seated and learn.

Suddenly the apostle walked past me and tossed a handkerchief directly into my space. Once I caught the handkerchief in the air the apostle said to me, "Acts 19:11–12. Read." Trusting him, I accepted the handkerchief and held it close to me as I was led of the Holy Spirit. The apostle then called for everyone to bring their children to him so that he could pray for them. He stated that the enemy was trying to mess with the children and that God's prayer would protect them. I hurried to put my smallest baby in my arms and asked the older children to get up with me so that they could receive prayer.

My husband resisted this idea and told me that I could go up for prayer but I could not take his children. Confused about his hostility toward a harmless prayer, I asked him why? His response was that the church was a scam and that he had seen lots of preachers like this one.

He refused my efforts and fought me in every way. My understanding was that this church would be a safe place. I could feel it. Besides my friend the Holy Spirit was there; he met me at the door. I believed that my answers were in this church, if I could only hold on a little longer. Taking a deep breath of relief, I said to the Lord, *I am home.*

There was a tugging at in my insides that confirmed for me that I needed to be in that prayer line with my children. I grabbed one son and went quickly to the line. I was worried that they would stop praying before I got up there. I had spent nearly fifteen minutes going back and forth with my husband about if the children could pray at this church.

Standing in front of the apostle with my son, he placed oil on his head. As I began walking away he urgently called me back and placed oil on my head as well. He stated that although he was only praying for children the Holy Spirit asked him to pray for me as well.

The authority and power that came forth from this man's mouth was impressive. He taught well and spoke a clear message of Jesus the Christ. Since the Holy Spirit had been so kind to me I wanted to please him. I began thinking to myself, I think that I will give this church a try.

The apostle walked past my row and looked directly at me and said, "this won't work". At the time I did not understand what he was saying to me. Quietly I sat and allowed my heart to listen to his words. It was then that I figured out what he was implying. My marriage was unhealthy and my change and coming back to the LORD would not survive with him in my life.

I knew in my heart that my marriage was a mess. I also knew that I needed to get out of the cult lifestyle. My husband was still in the cult and demanded that I remain connected as well. Just as the apostle said, this wasn't working. I realized it was true. Deep in my heart I knew my marriage was over. Still, I wanted to give it a chance to survive.

The service ended, and my burden was removed. While in the car my husband asked me what I had in my hand. I told him it was a handkerchief. Forcefully he opened my hands. When he saw the handkerchief, he demanded that I threw it away before we got home. I refused to throw it away. I explained to him how important it was that I keep it. At the time that I was defending my need for this handkerchief I had no idea what it was for. When I took the time to read the scripture that the apostle gave to me I learned something very important. The handkerchief was to protect me from evil spirits. The scripture states that Apostle Paul gave handkerchiefs to those who were sick and vexed with evil spirits.

My husband took my handkerchief and threw it out of the window. I no longer had the handkerchief because he took it but what he could not take from me was the lovely experience that I had at church and the biblical scripture that I had written down concerning the handkerchief.

While in the church the teaching remained biblical. Before long I began to understand the meaning of salvation. It made sense that mankind needed a savior. I understood that my good works alone did not please the LORD. My good works would not ensure eternal life.

After sitting under this healthy teaching, I made a clear decision to go full force and try this Christian way of living. I was going to serve the LORD in an effective way. I went to church every Sunday morning and after a while the message changed a little. The apostle went from teaching about salvation to talking about sin. The conversational biblical teaching on sin was very hard for me to listen to.

When he preached on sin I had a feeling that he was talking to me. In my heart I knew that this could not be true because I was not a sinner. The apostle beat on the subject so often that it became tiring. I did not want to hear about sin and all the sinners who committed sin each Sunday morning. In my eyes my life was clean. After all, I did not behave in the poor manner that the Christians did, I thought to myself. I did not do drugs, drink, or hurt people.

Since this was the case I was good in the LORDs eyes. The apostle continued doing what the LORD told him to do, deal with the topic of sin. It irritated me. It was a waste of my time. I did not come to church to hear about sin. I came to church to be healed completely. I came because the Holy Spirit asked me to. Not to listen to continual sermons on the sin of mankind.

The truth of the matter was that I was having a hard time grasping the fact that I was a sinner without salvation through Christ Jesus.

The teaching was so powerful that it began to not only deal with my flesh but also my mind. The sermons were cutting me deep in my heart and I came to realize that I needed to change my ways. Slowly, I realized that no matter how many great or kind things I did for others, I was still a sinner in God's eyes if I did not accept Jesus as my Lord and savior and work towards a life of holy living. I took my next step towards salvation through Christ Jesus, my beliefs changed.

CHAPTER 14

WHO IS SPEAKING?

When my family and I joined the church, I was told that the Christian way of life would take time to learn. I was told that people there would help me understand all that was taking place. Something intriguing took place within me every Sunday when I stepped into the church. I'd have this private moment with the Holy Spirit and I would say out loud, after taking a deep breath, "Daddy, I am home." I had never called the LORD Daddy before.

He was showing himself to me in a new light. He began revealing his many attributes to me. I no longer recognized him as the heavenly Father but as my one and only Father. Our relationship became more intimate. More that that, I felt like a child who submitted to Him, which caused me to call him Daddy, just as a child would. I was becoming aware of his different characteristics.

Now that I was no longer affiliated with this cult, I felt hopeful. I was hopeful that I would begin a brighter future and intimate relationship with the Father. In my hopefulness, it was unfortunate that I continued experiencing the side effects of life after the occult. Spending time with the Holy Spirit taught me that I could not depend upon my experiences, I needed to remain faithful to the scriptures. I needed to follow his leading. It was because of this that I decided to remain focus on reading my bible and faithfulness to the LORD. I believed that all would be well, but it was not. There were consequences for my lifestyle of sinful idol worship and I still needed to work through some things.

I had a lot to learn about the ways of the LORD. You see, our LORD expects for us to be obedient unto him. Just because I was not aware of the wrong that I had done, I was still held responsible for my actions. The Holy Spirit shared with me the biblical text of Hosea. In the fourth chapter of Hosea, the LORD expresses his disgust for the lack of healthy leadership of the priests. The people were supposed to be taught righteous living and holiness by the priests, but they were not. Instead they were being led astray and into unpleasant lifestyles. This angered the LORD and he sent Hosea to tell them of his anger. The people were not spared because of the lack of knowledge, and lack of good leadership. They too were held accountable for their actions. I can relate to this chapter. This was my confession to the LORD, "If I would have been properly taught by the church when I was young, I would have never taken this wrong turn in life". Since the church leadership did not teach me of the LORD, an agent of satan did. This was my reason for being led astray. Still, I suffered in the consequences of my actions.

One day while sitting in the congregation, I heard a voice telling me to go to the altar for prayer. I recognized this voice to be that of the LORD. I was obedient and attempted to walk to the front of the church. Suddenly, I heard another voice speak to me in a very convincing but bitter and sneaky tone. "Don't go up for that prayer!" the voice said. I recognized this voice as that of Lucifer. I realized I had a big problem on my hands. The voice that told me not to go was the voice that had ruled over me for many years. This voice pretended to be a friend of mine in many forms during many seasons of my life. At the time of the befriending, I was under the assumption that I was being assisted by a good and positive spiritual being. I was fooled.

Lucifer interrupted my peaceful walk towards the altar by telling me what he hoped would turn my heart away from the LORD. "It is his fault that you are in this big mess in the first place", he said. He was referring to my being untaught in the church and ignorant to biblical text.

Lucifer reminded me that I was among preachers but did not learn biblical truths but paraphrased stories of bible truths. I learned of the wickedness of their actions and unhealthy church leadership.

He reminded me of the LORD allowing his children in the church to mistreat me at the very young age of five years old. He reminded me of the reason I left the LORDs church and ended up with him and his demons as teachers and spiritual guides. He reminded me that he was there to help me when the church threw me away. He reminded me of the many teachers and spiritual guides that he sent my way to show me what I can do in the spiritual realm.

He said that it was them who taught me who I was when preachers had no idea and left me to fend for myself spiritually. Lucifer continued in his ranting while attempting to hold a convincing tone. He wanted to make it seem as if he was trying to help me avoid the big mistake of accepting the Lord Jesus into my life completely.

Determined to be with my Lord Jesus, I proceeded toward the front of the church. It was a struggle to go up and receive prayer after Lucifer's accusations against the LORD. With all my heart, I wanted to obey the Holy Spirit and stay in church to learn of Jesus and the bible.

I pressed my way forward with extreme mental force. Satan had a strong grip on my mind. I struggled against having anger toward the LORD. I struggled against blaming the LORD for all that I had suffered in the church because I was different. Time seemed to stand still. My ability to make a strong mental decision to fight back and remain in my relationship with the LORD was fading quickly. I became weak. I knew that I had to hurry and get to the altar before I changed my mind about receiving prayer.

Lucifer's plan was working. A renewed anger began to rise within me. I became angry about my past experiences within the church walls. It was true. The LORD had allowed me to be mistreated by his people. I was both tormented and upset as I was reminded of my pain. I was hoping that each step that I took showed the LORD how much I was trying to please him. Yet in my pressing forward and my obedience, lucifer did not stop reminding me. I was livid by the time I reached the altar.

I had finally made it to the altar and before the intercessors. Thankful to have made it, I was now being attacked in a different way. I refused to comply with the prayer. I did not want to participate. As a matter of a fact, I refused to follow the instructions of the intercessors. In anger I stood there not saying a word of what they wanted me to repeat. I changed my mind. I did not want to obey the LORD. I had gone through so many trails and schools seeking the LORD but knew him not. I had no biblical knowledge of him these years. I was the one who was lost in the shuffle. While growing up in church I was not taught about Jesus or salvation. I was taught about condemnation and the steps of obtaining low self-esteem in a place that was said to have been the house of God.

Standing before the altar I was furious! The LORD has allowed all of this and now my life was a mess! I had made a complete mess out of my life. Sitting in church I felt abandoned. I recalled being angry when others worshipped. In my opinion they understood the LORD, the teaching was passed down to them. I was expected to learn all on my own, thus I got lost.

As I recollected these thoughts, anger filled my heart. I became even more bitter and enraged. God had allowed all of this, and now I had served many gods. *I had made a mess out of my life*, I thought to myself. While sitting in church I felt abandoned by my true heavenly Father. I grew angry watching my brothers and sisters in Christ worship the true and living God that they had known all their lives. Jealousy filled my heart. Their knowledge of the biblical Jesus angered me.

Standing at the altar I had a private conversation with the LORD. Rhetorically I asked "do you mean that all of those years you watched me take the wrong turns and never stopped me? *I spoke with him concerning my belief that had Christians behaved as Jesus, I would not have strayed from him.*

If they had taught me properly I would have known that their God was the same as mine and I would not have had to leave the church. I would have known that their God was the one true God and not just some mean and horrible God connected to their church. I would have realized that, even though my experiences were very different from theirs, I still belonged in the church just the same, worshipping Jesus along with them.

I explained that I never would have thought Islam was pure and right. I would have never served in the army of Allah. I would never have chanted to false gods, nor worshipped statues. I would not have drunk from the cup of Isis and Osiris.

I went from serving one false god after another and it was all because of the church. After my conversation at the altar with the LORD, my battle worsened. *"Lift up your hands and ask for forgiveness,"* an intercessor said. Once I lifted my hands, she began saying the sinners' prayer. Forcefully pressing my way, I went through the entire prayer. I really did not want to do it. I did not want to open my mouth and willingly glorify the LORD.

By this time, I was emotionally burned out. "Say the name of Jesus" one of the mothers of the church said to me". Stubbornly I whispered, "Jesus." Struggling, I had gone through a whole emotional extravaganza. I was burned out from the emotional breaking of my mind. I was burned out from my past and current pain. *"Say the name of Jesus,"* one of the mothers of the church said to me. Stubbornly, I whispered *"Jesus"*. I could barely get his name out of my mouth. A mother of the church saw that I was struggling so she began coaching me. While she coached me, Lucifer continued talking to me. Repeatedly he said, "don't say it". I almost complied due to the amount of stress that I was under.

I was reluctant to respond properly. Another mother of the church commanded that I keep repeating the name Jesus. My heart was in bondage, and I struggled. It became even harder for me to speak the name Jesus from my lips. Finally, I heard the voice of my good friend the Holy Spirit speak to me *"Say the name Jesus one more time, and the devil won't bother you,"* he said. *This is my chance* I thought to myself. Rushing, I said the name Jesus out loud with great meaning.

"Call out the name Jesus," I heard the LORD say. I knew that this was my chance to get free. After calling out to Jesus my body began to jump extremely high. I had been tormented, and now the torment was being released from me. I was free. Lucifer was no longer reminding me about all my terrible life experiences with the church. He no longer reminded me about my past pain. My body was thrown all over the floor by the spirits that were being evicted from my body.

This process took many minutes. I was blinded during the whole process and could not see a thing. Later, I was told that the church members held hands in a circle to keep me from hurting myself. I was told that I became very strong and powerful. I was so strong that I could fling away the men who were trying to hold me. I don't remember that part, but I do remember feeling very powerful. I remember my voice sounding deep, like that of a man's.

I was told that I tossed men around in the front of the church. I was told that I became so strong that others from the congregation came forth joining hands to keep me safe. The prayer was over, and I felt great. No longer demonically oppressed because the spirits had been evicted. I rejoiced because I knew it was going to be a lovely day.

CHAPTER 15

BIBLE STUDY

It had been a while since I had recited the sinner's prayer and had decided to remain at the brick church for growth. I grew immensely and as I grew, my hunger for more of the word and greater understanding grew. This is what caused me to begin watching Christian television as a side dish to the teaching I received. I also met other believers who invited me to ministry events outside of the teaching of my apostle. I had agreed to stay at the church where I was sent and not to leave. So, I did not leave, I just visit other places as well as attending my home church. Trouble arose in my disobedience unto the Holy Spirit. I began having problems and spiritual warfare while reading the bible.

I became confused while reading biblical text. My study time with the Holy Spirit was not as effective and I misunderstood my lessons. The pleasantness that I had once enjoyed while reading the bible had now become a spiritual battle. Strange things began to happen to me when I read.

Lucifer recognized my dedication to the LORD and to my studies with the Holy Spirit. He tried to persuade me into losing focus on my goal of learning and being an effective servant. Daily I did my part. I studied and gave the Holy Spirit something to work with. I learned from the scriptures while at church and at home.

Demons stood against the wall and watched me read my bible. They stood purposely in a location that intimidated me. They would harass me. Some would come close to my face and study my reaction to their distracting behaviors. There was a demon that remained on the wall who would write with objects that was in hand. There were times when they would instigate fights between the children to distract me and then begin writing my response.

They would tell me that I was going to die. This was all done during my bible study with the Holy Spirit. This was distracting so yes, it worked. I was also bothered when reading the bible, the demons assigned to me made it appear, the words on the pages were changing.

If the bible stated, "Jesus is Lord and shepherd," once I began reading it would seem to state" Satan is our Lord and shepherd" or "Anu is our Lord and shepherd."

The words would change to benefit the cult or any of my other past ritual experiences of worship. This would make me anxious. I would become overwhelmed with stress. I would eventually be intimidated into ending my bible study with the Holy Spirit. Eventually my vision would be altered, and everything would go black. It would happen so quickly. I would feel a knock out as though I had been hit with a brick over the head.

For some reason I was still in a battle. I considered myself to be saved. I accepted Jesus as my Lord and savior. I was a tither and a participant in being a student of the word of the LORD, but I seemed to remain an open portal for demonic forces. I did not understand why I felt frustrated and hopeless because I was attending church faithfully, reading my Bible, and tithing regularly as I had been taught. Since Lucifer and his angels continued tormenting me and there was no intervention from the LORD my belief of faith became weary. I began to believe that I was not forgiven. I believed that God was angry with me.

I began to feel as though I should have just stayed in the occult since I remained suffering. The angels of the LORD who use to assist my every battle were no longer doing so. I felt alone in my struggle and I wanted to give up. But giving up was not an option for me because I loved the Holy Spirit too much to let go of him. He was my friend and confidant. He was my comforter and my teacher.

My attacks during bible study continued. I felt that I had strayed too far away for the LORD to want to help me. I almost submitted to the suffering believing that I would never be normal again. It appeared satan had control over it all. He was still ruining my life. Who knew, *maybe the LORD gave Lucifer permission to torture me some more;* I thought to myself. All I knew was that I was not going to give up on my new relationship with the KING of kings and LORD of Lords.

The Holy Spirit allowed me my time in my pity party. Afterwards we were back to studying, working hard and praying. I decided to pray a heartfelt LORD, please help me I feel like I am dying. Please keep the words in the bible from changing.

Even after my heartfelt prayers the words on the pages of my bible continued to scramble about. I did not give up but instead kept reading my Bible and having faith. I knew that one day this would end, and I would be okay. The Holy Spirit later explained to me the reason the words were scrambled on the pages of the Bible: I was still possessed by demons. Yes, I had received deliverance, but there was a process to my deliverance. I was not completely free of the demonic forces. My deliverance would come in stages. I had to deal with many demons and so within each season of my training with the Holy Spirit, I learned how to be set free.

Since the demons were still lodged inside me, they controlled my perception and eyesight. They controlled my body as well. Imagine having a huge ball of yarn with a tiny piece of lint in the middle of it. consider the real you being represented as a piece of lint and the entire ball of yarn that surrounds that lint represents the legions of demons oppressing you.

At the time of these incidents, the lovely Holy Spirit did not dwell inside of me. Closely he walked with me. He coached me and ministered to me. He helped me understand how to serve the LORD while in spiritual warfare. I was trained, taught, and given the grace to survive through my suffering, but I did not become filled with the Holy Spirit until long afterwards when my demonic oppression ended. The Holy Spirit encouraged me to keep pushing forward. Although I loved the LORD and had received Jesus as my personal savior, Lord over my life, I was still unclean. The Holy Spirit will not dwell in an unclean vessel.

CHAPTER 16

DECEPTION

Many years passed and I was doing well. Then, something happened. Mistakenly, I allowed Lucifer to deceive me again. His tactic was patience. Lucifer waited for the opportune time to launch his attack. His poison was rebellion, which is what he used to move me away from the LORD's will for my life.

My rebellion was not boldly handed over to me and this was Lucifer's trick. He was sneaky and very cunning. This was his trick. If I had been boldly rebellious it would have been obvious. I would have recognized it. I had already been trained how to fast and pray to kill my fleshly desires. I would have dealt very seriously with my flesh had I recognized my flesh rising in disobedience unto the LORD. Lucifer and his demons had been watching and charting on me and my reactions to his setups. This was Lucifer's trick. If I had been bold and rebellious, I would have noticed it myself and would have prayed and fasted. This rebellion was a silent killer. I say killer because it was sent to kill my divine destiny right before my eyes and with my participation.

Overwhelmed by boredom at my home church and under the leadership of my apostle I sought out other ministries for spiritual supplementation. The Holy Spirit specifically expressed to me that he wanted me to stay in the church with my apostle. I believed that television ministries had more to offer me. Especially the deliverance that I had been waiting for. I figured that it did not really matter where I went for spiritual growth since I was still learning. The main point the Holy Spirit was making was that he wanted me to go to a church and learn about Jesus biblically. I was doing so.

What I did not see during my rebellion was that Lucifer was attempting to get me away from my spiritual covering, my apostle. He was the only one whom the Holy Spirit spoke to concerning me and for very specific reasons. To avoid confusion was one of them. Because he said so was the other.

Before I was tempted by Lucifer, I had been completely pleased with my home church. I was pleased with the way my apostle delivered his sermons every Sunday. Then there came a time when I began to receive subliminal messages. These messages were so powerful that I could not fight them off, even when pleading the blood of Jesus. The messages were telling me of all the reasons that that I did not like my apostle, the church, or the members. The messages said I was bored and would learn better if I went to a different church.

Beelzebub came along and played upon my heart's desire to learn more. He knew that I was studious and loved to understand the how and why of a matter. Due to my experience with dealing with Beelzebub I knew better than to entertain him. What I knew to do was to ignore him and I was able to do this for a while. Over time the power struggle between Beelzebub and I became too much for me. I was not getting any assistance from the Holy Spirit during this time because I had done what he had asked me not to do but I did not realize it at the time. Therefore, Beelzebub was able to get in. He had to get me away from my safety net and my safety net is the Holy Spirit. When the time came that I could no longer bear the subliminal messages I gave in. Once the messages became too difficult for me to ignore, I came up with an excuse to visit other ministries and remain at my home church as well. In doing so I could claim that I was still following instructions.

I wanted to be delivered from dark spiritual forces. I had patiently waited for deliverance at my home church. I was growing in the word, but healing was not fully manifested in my life. My rebellion birthed manipulation. I had a plan. If I followed my plan exactly, I would be able to obey the Holy Spirit and still be just a little disobedient.

You see, if I went to every single service, did not miss one payment of tithes and volunteered to help whenever needed, I would still be obedient. You see, my way of thinking was that I had not really missed any church services. When I visited these other places because my church was closed by then. We had already gone home for the day.

This I know. To comfort my lie, I placed an excuse around my wrong doing. I was still learning as the Holy Spirit requested. I thought that I would get away with it. It amazed me to understand that he knows me. Even in my deepest secret of thought, he was on to my deception. Somehow, even in my knowing of his great wisdom I attempted to find cause to go to other ministries without permission. The only thing that could possibly go wrong is that the Holy Spirit would recognize that I knew exactly what he had originally instructed me to do. stay put.

I made it my prerogative to visit churches where he asked me not to go. Well, he didn't say not to visit the other ministers. What he said was I should stay at the ministry where he'd had placed me. In my desperate thinking, I had the little wiggle room that I needed so that I could claim that I had misunderstood. In the end, I paid a serious price for my actions.

I only shared this with you as a warning to you ahead of time. Obey the Holy Spirit. There is a reason for everything that he tells you to do. When you are stuck and feel lost, remember that he knows all things. He will help you out of your circumstances if you allow him to and if you are obedient always.

I learned that there is no such thing as partial obedience. We are obedient, or we are not. When I disobeyed, I was disrespecting our heavenly Father. No matter how much I sugarcoated it, the fact remains. Due to my disobedience, Beelzebub was allowed access into my life. I became confused in the teaching of other ministers and I believed that everyone else was right and that my apostle was wrong. I did not want to feel this way about my home church or my apostle.

Since Lucifer had a real hold on my mind I felt awkward about biblical teachings. Each day, hour, and second, I fought the demonic forces connected to my past. This battle seemed ongoing. The LORD used my apostle to bring me far in understanding his word. I hated the way that I was behaving towards him and his church.

Stuck in the confusion caused by my disobedience I began another battel. There was a catastrophe and one disaster after another. Satan was ruthless in his tactics he did not fight fair. I knew this but tried avoiding giving him credit for having power over my life. I was suffering because I was disobedient. I brought this on myself. The spirit of confusion consumed me. I went from blaming myself and then freeing myself from guilt. Too many years had past and I was still undelivered.

I did not want to keep going through satans traps, old attacks, and manipulations. In saying this, my actions of disobedience embraced this suffering because my unwillingness to do right caused it. I listened to so many preachers that I had become confused. I did not know who to believe. I learned that not all ministers teach alike. Many of them do not believe the same things about the bible. Different ministers have different battles and different wisdom from the LORD. Being spiritually fed by several men and women of the LORD caused me to become spiritually sick. I struggled receiving teaching from within the walls of my home church.

This would not have happened to me had I obeyed the Holy Spirit and stayed put, I thought to myself. The Holy Spirit knew what was best for me. He knew that a lot of garbage was being taught by false prophets. He tried to protect me. I did not listen to him and I ran out alone and into many pastures and grazed there anyway.

The lovely Holy Spirit was so patient with me. He refused to make me obey him. He also refused to allow me to move forward in spiritual growth. I thought that I had a better plan than the Holy

Spirit. In this, he reminded me that If I did not learn and do as he instructed me, I would fail in the end. When I did, he would just watch me fall and wallow in my tears. After a season in which he chose, he would remove me from my spiritual grave, he would give me grace and set me free from that bondage. He would put me back on the correct track and allow me to start over again, working towards a life of obedience.

He knew what I was after. I wanted to receive my deliverance and to then go back to my earlier years with him. Lessons and the miracles that I had experienced with him during my youth. He shared with me that this was a new season in my life and that it was not time and I needed to be patient. I had to wait until that season was available unto me. I had to grow up both mentally and spiritually. I had to obey leadership long term. I had to obey the commands of the LORD, always before experiencing that season again.

No matter how much he loved me, he couldn't allow me to do what I wanted to do. He had to put his foot down and be hard on me in these matters. I had to be obedient and stay put. I was learning the hard way. My training was exhausting.

As time went on, I became very spiritually ill. I was sorry I had disobeyed. I was very foolish, and God used some personal situations to show me right from wrong. He showed me why I would not grow while I was walking in disobedience. Eventually, I realized this to be true.

The Holy Spirit gave to me this comparison. He said, if you have just given birth and afterwards give the baby breastmilk, it is fine. Now, what would happen if at the next feeding, you gave the newborn an artificial formula purchased in a store? What if at the next feeding, you fed the baby soy formula and then went back to breast milk? What do you think will happen?

I thought about it and this is my conclusion. The newborns digestive system would become confused. This would cause a problem and the baby would begin to vomit. This is what happened to me. He was showing me that therefore I became sick in the spirit realm. I was feeding off so many different teachings.

Understand that the anointing is like a medicine. Teaching is strategic. A minister attempts to get across a point that is necessary for that individual flock, not for everyone. Since I had so many different ministers teaching me and speaking over my life, I had more than one anointing dealing with my situations. Since the teaching wasn't specifically for me and the anointing present and assigned to that house was not effective for me, my spirit became confused and sick. My demonic warfare increased.

Many ministers were giving me advice, saying boldly that this is what the LORD had said. The Holy Spirit taught me that this was not healthy and that everyone was not being honest with me about their prophecy. The Holy Spirit taught me through tough love. Not to be mean but to show me that he knew what was best. During this time, he also showed me that it was always best to know the LORD for myself. The Holy Spirit knew that my home church was where I should be taught and trained. He showed me that he had a reason for sending me there. He also knew that my home church wasn't perfect by far, but I was to stay there for a reason and a season. I later found out why he had sent me to this ministry.

My home church was a major place of holiness and discipline. The Holy Spirit knew that I needed to succeed in ministry and walk out a life full of true holiness. While at this church I obtained tough skin, in a spiritual sense. This tough skin protected me from being hurt whenever I was rebuked or held responsible for an action that I did or did not do but was accused of. It prepared me for the living of a lifestyle of holiness which was required of me. It was a strict house where the LORD spoke, and the presence of the LORD dwelled.

It is the goal of Lucifer to remove you from the church intended for you to train for a future ministry. Once he has you cornered in a life of willing and knowledgeable disobedience he has almost reached his goal. He does this so it will be difficult for you to grow properly in the things of God. Lucifer desires to destroy the church; he does this through encouraging preachers in providing vain teachings and false biblical interpretations. Many churches are teaching things that are not scriptural. We must be watchful of false teachers who claim to come in the name of our LORD.

My friend, the LORD allows us to go through trials and tribulations. This does not mean that he does not love us. Jesus is our shepherd, and he will allow us to go through trials and tribulations every day if that is what is necessary for our growth. When we steer away from his loving arms, tribulations help us to stay where he has placed us. Our Good Shepherd will lead us to green pastures. He will lead us to even greener pastures, if we allow him to and stop getting in his way. Do yourself a favor and decide to stay where the LORD has placed you to learn of his word. In that place, we can truly learn from the Holy Spirit. It is then that our LORD will get out of us what he truly desires. This is what I called my time of learning. This is the place in which the Spirit of the LORD prepares us to walk in our true and divine purpose.

CHAPTER 17

INTRUDER

By this time, I had gone through numerous overwhelming spiritual attacks. Beelzebub came there to threaten me with the spirit of fear one night. When he appeared to me I was not too concerned. I had grown a lot by this time. I was used to the back and forth struggle with Beelzebub. Several times he attempted to come back into my life. Many times, he attempted to manipulate me. He would say negative things about Christianity to cause me to doubt what I believed. Beelzebub kept asking me to come back to what he called "the truth" and leave all the false religion alone. He offered me power and authority over the world and court systems in the spirit realm. He said that he had a place for me to walk in great power and authority if I wanted it.

Although he continued to try to tempt me, I refused him time and time again. There was no room for temptation in my life since Beelzebub had nothing I desired. I was now at home with my LORD and that was where I would stay. I refused and continued to serve my Lord and Savior Jesus Christ. I was dedicated. I could not be easily fooled by the tactics of satan any longer. One evening while on an assignment I desired a midnight snack. There was a vending machine nearby where I could make a purchase. Walking towards the vending machine the angels of the LORD assigned to me revealed themselves. Once they revealed themselves they went on continuing to protect me. They held hands and surrounded me, as I walked they moved with me keeping me enclosed in the circle.

Once Beelzebub saw the angels of the LORD, he revealed himself as well. Attempting to intimidate me, he lit up very brightly and then went dim. He wanted me to see him watching me. I remained calm and unafraid. I made my purchase and walked away to sit down. Shortly after sitting I went into a trance. While in this trance, I could feel oil dripping over my head which began to stream down my face and onto my neck. To be clear, the oil that I was feeling poured onto me was in the spirit realm. I could feel it in the flesh. While in the trance I heard the angels of the LORD praying for me. They began cheering me on. They said "Mattia, you won the fight". They were so happy for me. Some gave the LORD glory while others continued cheering me on. The LORD continued to get glory for my victory.

During all this excitement and cheers of celebration I was confused. I did not understand why the angels of the LORD were celebrating my winning a fight when I had not been in any fight. Not one that I was aware of anyway. As for them cheering concerning my victory, I was not sure what that was all about. It seemed as if I had been away from the physical realm of my flesh for a long time. When I came out of the trance I looked at the clock and according to the clock I was in the trance for maybe twenty minutes.

Time in the spirit realm is very different than in the physical realm. It seemed that I was gone a lot longer than twenty minutes due to all that I had accomplished while away. A lot can be done in the timing of the realm of the spirit. As I listened to the angels cheer me on I became excited as well. For I had won a fight of the unknown. I continued to listen to them give glory to God for my victory.

Once the angels of the LORD awakened me from the trance, I got up and walked into a room. As I walked into the room a change took place in its' atmosphere. A great peace was present. I witnessed what looked like heaven coming down to earth and into the room where I stood. Even though I was awake and in present time, I could tell that I was seeing in the spirit realm and not in the natural. I saw the open vision as in a solid form. It was shown to me in this matter so that I would understand that it was a spiritual matter, but it was given a solid for the sense of reality so that I would take this vision very seriously. I witnessed the ceiling open and I saw the throne of the LORD. Jesus was sitting with the Father and they were being lowered into the room through the open space. When this happened, I became afraid and my heart started to race. I screamed and once I did the vision seemed to evaporate. I couldn't believe it. I saw God's glory come down along with the throne and a part of heaven. The Holy Spirit saw how frightened I was and closed my visibility While explaining to me that it was not the LORD's intention for me to be frightened but only to see his glory.

Hours later while driving home I witnessed the protection and being surrounded by the angels of the LORD. I felt safe and went to sit on the couch to get some rest. It was then that my son stood in the doorway of his bedroom and starred at me. He then looked back at the door. Looking back and forth from the door to me he said, "mommy there is a dark man at the door".

Looking at the door, I witnessed Beelzebub standing there. I could only assume that he was speaking of Beelzebub. He had followed me home attempting to fight with me. He wanted to distract me from my victory and take me through an unnecessary trial so that I could be set back from all that I had gained in the spirit realm while away with the LORD. He wanted to kill my confidence in the victory that I had already won. He came to my home, invading my place of peace and security seeking to place fear in me. I knew that the angels of the LORD were with me, so I was confident. I replied to my son letting him know that I saw him as well. "Go and get ready for school baby, mommy has to pray "I said. Immediately I went into prayer. I was exhausted from a long night and was ready to go to bed. Once again, I had a fight on my hands.

I was exhausted with spiritual warfare. This back and forth deliverance process was real work. I was frustrated. I just wanted to move forward with my life. I was at my wit's end and this deliverance issue was like a never ending story. In my heart and mind, I had enough already. I was no longer living a life of idol worship or deep dangerous meditations. I had left my dark past alone. *So, what's the big deal?* I said to my LORD. People worship idols and sin every single day; so why was Satan continually harassing me. It was enough already! I grabbed the telephone to call my pastor. I needed him to pray for me and perhaps give me some guidance about what I was supposed to do next.

I needed answers concerning exactly how long this thing called deliverance would take. Desperate, I needed to hear a time frame for the ending period of this torment. I needed guidance. While the telephone rang I began to do my part which was to speak biblical truths concerning my life. I declared Jesus had conquered all sickness and disease. I declared the blood of Jesus that had been shed for the sins of mankind. I declared that I agreed and claimed the benefits of salvation through Jesus the anointed one. The apostle's wife answered the telephone. I greeted her and asked to speak with the apostle. She asked me what was wrong, telling me that he was out. I explained to her that Beelzebub was in my house. I gave her the details. I told her that I needed to ask him how long this deliverance was going to take.

She told me that there was nothing that she could do for me. She explained how they had prayed for me and had laid their hands upon me as the bible suggested. She explained that I had been through a lot and had to be delivered. She told me that deliverance could take a while to be completed. I thanked her and hung up. I began to cry. I figured that I should ask for forgiveness again, so I went into conversational prayer and spoke with the LORD concerning my suffering. The Holy Spirit explained to me that I had a lot to learn. He told me that I was still learning, and I needed to learn what real deliverance was. I said okay. I told him that I was willing to learn and to go through the process. Yes, I was extremely tired. but I continued to press my way and do what the Spirit of the LORD suggested.

Dear friend, I have found that deliverance means to be brought out of something, to be delivered out of a thing, place, or situation. I was discouraged because I prayed as the Christians had taught me. I fasted as the Spirit of the LORD instructed me. I remained demonically bound.

As soon as I lay down to get some rest Beelzebub walked over to me. While surrounded by angels of the LORD, Beelzebub leaned over the couch and got inside of me. It felt like I was putting on a snow suit. He put his legs in and cozied his way inside of me, squishing around. He placed his arms inside of mine and then wiggled around, trying to fit in perfectly. Once inside I seemed to go into a trance and could not move. Demons followed suite, continuing to get inside of me until there were nine comfortably lodged inside. I thought very quickly because I was overwhelmed. My mouth was controlled by the demonic forces so I could not speak. I figured that I could speak internally to my spirit within my mind. This was my prayer, "*LORD, if there is anything in me that is not like you, please, take it away.*" The minute I thought those words, the angels of the LORD began pushing on my belly.

They pushed on my navel, and once again the demonic forces went out of me and left my home. When the angels pushed on my belly, I felt pain around my navel. There was a popping sound; and then each demon squealed as it came out. There was an angel on each side of me and one above my head. They pushed on my stomach and again there was a loud pop and a squeal. It felt like there was a ripping taking place, as though a tick had latched onto my insides and was being pulled out through my navel. I suffered from this type of situation quite often, but in several different forms.

I witnessed demonic spirits following me everywhere I went during this season. They watched me and seemed to study my every move, which was very aggravating. Although this was a long and frustrating season of my life, I continued to pray and worship the LORD. I was determined to trust him for my deliverance.

CHAPTER 18

POSSESSED

It was late in the evening when my family and I returned home from an outing. We'd had a wonderful evening together; we were tired and ready to get inside and call it a night. The children got out of the car and went into the house. I could hear them from the driveway, saying, "Yuck, Mommy! Ew! What's in here?" I walked in after them, and I got sick to my stomach. I thought I would vomit.

The children said, "Mommy, this house is making me sick. What's in here?" I looked toward the back hallway and saw twelve demons. It appears they were coming from my bedroom. They wore very dark, black garments, and they were very dark as well. Thump, thump, thump. I could hear them marching. Their marching was both solid sounding and loud. They sounded like soldiers marching on pavement. I watched these demons march through my entire house. They went from one end of the house to the other. Their marching was loud in the spirit realm, and I could hear them chanting in a language that I did not know.

Their energy and the atmosphere were so demonic that it seeped out like smoke from a burning furnace. It smelled like burning carcasses. They spoke in tongues and in a kind of song-chant. I was overwhelmed, and I told the children to get ready for bed, that it was late, and I needed to seek the LORD's direction. Immediately, the Spirit of the LORD reminded me about the scripture that says God inhabits the praises of his people. At that moment, I began to sing songs that glorified Jesus. I worshiped the Lord for what seemed to be an eternity with great passion, adoration, and love from way down in my heart. I thought that it would be best if I stayed in the living room, which was close to the children's bedroom. I needed to be close to them in case they cried out.

Grabbing my stomach, I slouched over the armrest of the couch because I could no longer stand up. The demons had totally overpowered me. I lay on the couch and sang songs of praise. Suddenly, the presence of evil grew even the stronger. It seemed as though the demons were not intimidated by my worship or my Lord Jesus. The presence of evil was so strong, it made me not only sick but very weak. Still, I kept singing praises unto the Lord.

when I felt as though there would be no change an angel suddenly appeared in the middle of my living room floor. There she was. A beautiful, huge angel she was large and lovely. She spoke to the chief demon in an authoritative tone of voice: "You have to leave. "The chief demon replied, "Where can we go?" The angel of the LORD said, "I don't care where you go, but you have to get out of here!" The demons left in such speed that to say immediately would be almost too long. Time is so strange in the supernatural realm. It is best to express their quick departure by saying that they vanished. My home became livable once again, and I was at peace. I rejoiced out loud as well as within my heart. The angel of the LORD said I should rest because the demons would be back to try me again. She said if I wasn't strong enough to endure on the next time around, I would not be able to protect my house and my children.

I listened carefully to what she said, and I told the Lord thank you. I gave the angel my thanks, and she said "All thanks belonged to Jesus, who died upon the cross for your deliverance to take place and for others who would come for deliverance afterward." She gave me her blessing of peace upon my house, and I went to sleep right away.

CHAPTER 19

LEAVING

While sitting in church one Sunday morning, I heard an announcement that there would be Saturday morning prayer at 7:00 a.m. I was very excited and decided that I would be there, front and center. Things were going well for me by this time. I was very happy and my relationship with the LORD was amazing!

Each day, I grew in the wisdom of holy living. I was constantly learning more about Jesus Christ and his message to the world. I indulged in his presence excessively. This new feeling that I had for the Lord Jesus was as one who is head over heels in love. I never had this great desire for Jesus before. I knew of him and even had personal experiences which caused me to have feelings of kindness towards him. I just did not have that deep-rooted love for him.

I believe that my relationship with the Lord Jesus was like that of a child that grows up having a nanny taking care of their needs. In cases like these, the child begins to lean toward the nanny for everything and sometimes loses the close relationship with her birth mother. Jesus was in my life as a child but since I depended upon the angels of the LORD and the Holy Spirit for everything, I felt closer to them.

Growing up being hurt in the church caused me to miss the understanding of biblical scripture. I was always at war spiritually and not able to sit and be nurtured within the walls of the church. This lack of teaching was what caused me to miss what the LORD wanted to show me concerning Jesus. I was puzzled when I heard people say how much they loved Jesus. I could not comprehend this type of love but desired it. Over time and through building the relationship, I too fell in love with the Lord Jesus. It was a process.

I began to experience this love when I took the time to do things that caused me to grow tremendously in the things that concerned the LORD. Daily I spent time with the Holy Spirit. I made a point to learn how to practice the things that the Holy Spirit taught me.

Since the week had come to an end and Saturday was just a day away I decided to go bed early so I would not be late. I have learned that being late can distract others and disturb the atmosphere. Saturday morning arrived, and I was ready for this new season of learning prayer in my life. I got out of my car and went into the church to join the others.

Once inside, we greeted one another with great big hugs and lots of smiles. It was an awesome time and I was enjoying myself. Prayer went on for a while and then things became intense. It was then that a male minister went around the sanctuary prophesying to some of the people. He spoke claiming that his words were from the LORD.

I was familiar with prophecy and therefore comfortable and unoffended. Things were going well until the minister walked over to me and laid his hand upon my forehead and began to speak into my life. He said "the Lord wants you to get closer to him. The Lord said that you are far from him and that you need God."

Confused I began thinking to myself, *what is going on?* Within the blink of an eye, I saw myself in the spirit realm being raped by demons. In the spirit realm, I witnessed my clothes being taken off, one item at a time in a violent manner. This was not a real-life occurrence but a spiritual one. I realized that I was under another demonic attack. Everything went black and I went into a trance. When I came back to myself, I grabbed my things and ran out of the church. I remember crying for days. I was very emotional over this manipulation that took place at the devil's hands.

I was hurting emotionally because an evil spirit had been transferred and deposited into my body by a minister of the gospel. I did not know that this was possible. Once I got home I threw my bible and anything that had anything to do with the gospel and threw it in the garbage. I went around a raging wolf inside. My flesh was once again possessed by demons.

I told an associate of mine what happened to me. While speaking with him, he looked at me with a glare in his eyes. I recognized that glare because I recognized the spirit that possessed it. It was the spirit that I had once been manipulated into believing was a spiritual authority. Within this manipulation I adapted to love and trust him. He is a deceptive spirit and his name is Beelzebub. Many years prior, Beelzebub portrayed himself kind spiritual being who only desired to help me know and understand God and his precepts.

I was in a spiritual rage and decided that Christianity was no longer for me. While I went through this rage I remained possessed for several weeks. Within my being possessed my spirit found a way to fight on my behalf. I can only believe that this was the reason that deep inside I continued to pray and trust that God would deliver me. There was somehow a strength that fought back against the demonic forces that were overpowering me. Somehow, I was keeping the faith.

Then one day the angels of the LORD pressed on my belly and released the spirits from my body. I was no longer tormented by this group of demonic forces, but this was only for a short time. I must tell you that my battle has been long and extremely hard. My friend, allow me to tell you this. Not all ministers will give you a tormenting spirit as I was given. If you recall in a previous chapter I explained that Beelzebub had been trying to possess me for some time. He wasn't as successful as he had hoped because I was an unwilling participant. This time he was able to gain access to me because it was a willing transfer on my part.

You see, I allowed this minister of the gospel to lay his hands upon me because I trusted him. He was a minister of the gospel. The apostle left him in charge of the service. I was at Saturday morning prayer. What could possibly go wrong? I didn't know that a minister of the gospel could transfer demons. Remember I was new to Christianity in terms of biblical understanding. Allow me to inform you that a man or woman who professes to know the Lord Jesus but continues to live a double lifestyle is a very dangerous vessel in the church. These ministers are not only dangerous to themselves, they are a walking, ticking time bomb against the clergy and anyone else who is connected to them. If an individual is not filled with the Holy Spirit, he has no control over when or how an evil spirit will use him as a vessel.

In times past Beelzebub couldn't get inside of me because I was expecting him. I was prepared, and I had my guard up. It was when I put my guard down and was just a happy-go-lucky woman, ready to pray at church that he made his move against me. After this took place, I stayed away from church for a while. When a coworker of mine asked me why I had not been back to church, I informed her that I would not be going back. I couldn't explain everything to her because she most likely wouldn't have understood. But I told her what I thought she could grasp spiritually without making her confused. She advised me to continue coming to church to learn of the Lord. I understood what she was saying but needed time to heal. Besides, how would I build up enough trust to go back into the church building again? The man that transferred the demonic spirit to me was a licensed minister of our church who taught that day. The pastor had a secret life. He was unclean and should not have been laying hands on anyone during prayer. The Holy Spirit revealed my situation to my apostle concerning this man's secret life and for a season he was removed from his ministerial duties so that he could get his life cleaned up.

As time went on, somehow, I came to a place emotionally where I had enough strength to say my usual prayer: "LORD, if there is anything inside me that is not like you, please remove it." I also asked

God for forgiveness for anything I may have done that I was unaware of. I asked him to please help me, and again the demonic forces were ripped out of my navel when the angels of the LORD pressed on my stomach. As the angels pushed hard, the demons came out, each one making pop and squealing sounds. This was extremely painful. I felt totally drained and exhausted afterwards.

Once I received my freedom from these demonic spirits, I knew that I had to get it together. I had to get back to my secret place with the Holy Spirit so that we could continue in my training. To prepare for our reunification I needed to purchase a bible and study materials all over again because during my rage I threw everything pertaining to Jesus away. Once mentally restored I was ready and willing to continue my journey.

CHAPTER 20

DISOBEDIENCE

This level of demonic possession was more strategic. The purpose of the attack was to cause me to be a Christian of poor character. During this time my only concern was what the LORD said to me. Anything else was of no importance. It is healthy to desire hearing the voice of God for oneself. That is not a problem. Being arrogant and not being willing to listen to the shepherd sent to watch over your soul is where the problem lays. This demonic influence is a scheme satan uses to build pride in an individual and to cause one to be alone. In their aloneness is where he often defeats them. It is during this time that a spirit of confusion manifests in the person's life

When oppressed with a spirit confusion, distraction will follow. This demon possessed individual will place themselves front and center within the walls of the church. They must be seen so that they can distract the congregation. With this distraction the LORD is not glorified completely. The church is supposed to be a place of peace, but mockery and discomfort will be present when this individual is at work. The people desire to experience the peace and comfort of the LORD. It is unlikely to happen in this type of atmosphere. Learning from the sermon taught is less likely to take place and the evil spirit achieves its goal.

It is important for demons to hinder any move the Holy Spirit needs to make. Weak spiritual leadership will not confront this evil spirit, and the individual that is being used will remain possessed and become even more prideful and unwilling to submit. Of course, it is important that the message of the LORD not come from the pulpit. This is Satan's purpose in using this individual.

Possessed individuals never want to hear what the pastor says concerning the things of the LORD. They will not be ashamed to admit this. One of their tactics is to distract others with conversation while service is taking place. They say things like "I don't agree with what he is preaching, do you?" They do this to distract you from listening to the sermon. Their plan is to make you feel the same way they do about the pastor. They want you to leave the church and follow them into a bitter wilderness. It is because of this that I was taught not to distract others when they are listening to the sermon. Therefore, without being rude, I try not to tell my neighbor things while preaching is taking place. I know that it is popular in church culture today, but it can be distracting. It is important to remain focused on the message being taught from the pulpit if we are to be effective servants of the LORD.

They say, "I do not have to listen to him. I can read the Bible for myself." If you ever encounter such a possessed individual rebuke the evil spirit right away. If you do you will learn and grow spiritually from the lesson being taught. Remember, it is important that you be strong and fight for yourself in this type of situation. Remember, to rebuke the evil spirit and not the person. There is a difference.

Do your best not to allow Lucifer to disrespect the LORD's order to things. Never be intimidated by unclean-spirit-filled people, but be wise in your dealings with them. It is important that they let you know why you do not need to be in the church. Stand your ground and focus on why you are there. Do not allow them to deposit their negativity in your heart and mind.

There was a time in my life when I was approached by a demonic spirit who went by the name Belial. He tried to explain to me why I did not need to attend church service. During this time, the Holy Spirit was training me in spiritual warfare. He taught me about the demons, their titles, and their assignments. He taught me how to deal with each demon. Belial knew about my training and attempted to manipulate me away from my lessons with the Holy Spirit. He told me that I did not need to learn the Lord's way and that I could learn on my own. That was a lie. It was necessary for me to be in a healthy church, learning about Jesus. It was important for me to be part of the body of believers. It was important that I was joined in a church and not out in the world alone trying to figure out the things of God.

It was Belial's plan to divide and conquer. He wanted to remove me from my spiritual covering. After a long battle in my mind, he eventually succeeded in removing my desire to be in the church for a long time. He also removed the joy that I once felt about being in the church. He failed to remove me from the church, but I had very little joy while I was there. I still desired to know the Lord and have fellowship with the Holy Spirit. We continued our relationship but I wanted nothing to do with the people who falsely worshipped in the church. I had enough of their drama. Although they had their drama going on, I was the one who was out of order. Out of confusion I was unable to see this. We all had our own issues, but I was possessed myself and should have been looking at myself and the drama I now brought to the table. I did not recognize this as my personal issue at the time. In my misery I received a direct order from the Lord, which was to keep my eyes on him and not be sidetracked by the warfare that was coming my way. I was forewarned. I was to walk in the love of God. I was to keep my eyes on the Lord and listen to the Holy Spirit's instructions. He said, do not look at the people, look directly at me. But I didn't, I was distracted by the drama that was around me. The church gossip, the I don't like you, you can't join my choir nonsense and so much more. My disobedience to the direct order of the Holy Spirit cost me dearly. I did not pass the test placed before me. Not passing my test caused me to be hindered.

My advice to you is, keep your eyes on the Lord. Turn a blind eye to the distractions around you. When you witness things taking place that are out of order just pray. Ask the Holy Spirit for the power to overcome them. When you do this, you will be able to pass your Holy Spirit given test and move forward. Remember that Jesus is rooting for you. He is cheering you on. He knows that you will succeed. You will make it. He will not ask you to do something that you cannot do. He is not that type of Savior.

CHAPTER 21

GREATEST DESIRE

While I was sitting in church one day, I told the LORD that I was very hungry for him. I told the LORD that I didn't want to sit down and be an ordinary Christian.

I wasn't satisfied with clapping my hands and stomping my feet in church. I wasn't happy going to one service after another and leaving still feeling as though I was missing something. God is good; he gave me just what I asked him for, which was much more of him. He blessed me so with more of his presence. At the time, I had no idea of the price that I would have to pay to get closer to Him.

During my training with the Holy Spirit, I walked through many difficult situations. I gained a lot of insight, and most of all, I learned that Jesus was powerful. He was more powerful than the previous spiritual practices I had encountered in my past. I learned a lot and my relationship with the Holy Spirit grew. I trusted him to assist me in every life decision that I made. I grew to love him more and our bond became stronger.

CHAPTER 22

BROKENNESS

I made a decision to either submit totally to the LORD or stay broken, angry and run away from him. The Bible tells us there is no place we can go to hide from the LORD. He is always around; he is omnipresent. My previous attempts to run and hide from him were not successful. I realized it was better to always submit to his will for my life.

Coming to the decision to submit I saw the need to change my surroundings. I had to put myself in a place with people who understood where the Holy Spirit was taking me spiritually. These people helped me to see that it was not that life was unfair to me. It was that in each season we go through tests and trails. These tests and trials show us what we are capable of. They also show us what we need if we are to gain spiritual strength.

I did not sit around sulking during this time. It would not have helped my situation at all. Instead, I learned my next level of fasting and prayer. This consisted of fasting for longer and drinking only water. It consisted of going on complete dry fasts which meant that I would consume nothing for many days. I had to do this because I had witnessed Satan on a new level. I had no idea of his ability to touch the life of a dedicated believer. I was experiencing more than the average preacher teaches about. Since this was the case there was no reference point that I could use during this point in my life.

I was enrolled in the school of the Holy Spirit. Through my personal experiences, the LORD was teaching me about the ways of the enemy. This was not an easy school. At times, I wanted to drop out and forget about my desire to know more about the LORD.

During my training, I suffered in agony. I was anguished. I was overwhelmed by the voices of demons. It was an uncontrollable experience. Being taunted by demons brought on an anxiety attack. I became sick to my stomach. I experienced what seemed to be large stabbing pains in my head. My whole body ached. I was mentally tormented.

The apostle whose tutelage I was under watched my situation. He was not able to interfere. He knew that I needed to walk through this situation with the Holy Spirit for spiritual strengthening. The Holy Spirit was teaching me how to depend solely upon him concerning my lessons of spiritual warfare.

One Sunday morning, while sitting quietly in the congregation, I was under attack and became overwhelmed. I was so distraught that while he was preaching I got on my knees and prayed silently with my cloth over my head. My apostle saw that I was suffering and struggling in my fight and said out loud from the pulpit, "If any intercessors want to pray for Mattia, you may do so."

Not one of the intercessors came but I could hear them from where I kneeled. They were mumbling statements like, I am not praying for her. While on my knees I prayed. Then said "Lord, how do we have intercessors and licensed ministers who are afraid of praying away demonic spirits?" I could not believe that ministers of the Gospel were afraid of spiritual warfare. I promised myself that very day that once I had been delivered and was strong I would always be prepared to do battle on behalf of others struggling under demonic oppression. I promised myself that I would never leave them alone on the battlefield; if it was the LORDs will for me to get involved.

The training that I received after passing this test was horrific, intense, and exhausting. Demons prophesied to me both spiritually and subliminally. Satan assigned different demons into my life for different purposes. My body reacted as satan instructed by way of demonic prophecy. I received messages from satan and then he would insert himself into my spirit causing me to go into a trance. His demons had access to me in this way as well. Making me susceptible to his will. Holding my head in both hands I would scream "Stop speaking into my life!"

I eventually learned that Satan would not have mercy upon me because I was suffering. In fact, my admission that I was suffering only gave him pleasure and proved that what he was doing in my life was working.

I learned something very important concerning warfare. When I revealed that I was overwhelmed more force was placed upon my mind.

Beelzebub threatened me. He told me that if I remained in the church I would die. He placed horrible pain upon me while I was sitting in the church. He would then say, leave, leave now. When I did not leave he would subject me to terrible mental torment. He stated that he would stop if I left the church. When I did not comply he would release a spirit of confusion upon me. This was not one spirit; it came in a team. Confusion needs to be represented in a confusing way. One demon cannot effectively confuse you; this was explained to me during my training with the Holy Spirit. There is a strategy to confusing a person. The more demons available for this task, the better.

One of the feelings that I had when I was attacked by the spirit of confusion was that knives were being forced through my head. I thought I was being stabbed in my head continually. The punctures felt real and was horrifying. During these stabbing pains all the demons assigned to me would talk at once. They would say different things and ask me questions. Each demon would ask a different question at the same time. Each voice was different, and sometimes it would be the voice of someone I knew to make the experience more hurtful. This brings about a sense of paranoia. You believe that the people who you know, and trust have betrayed you. It is a trick of the adversary to isolate you.

I believe that the stabbing pains were a way to urge me to answer the questions rapidly. Rapidly answering a bunch of questions that make no sense or have no connection to each other is confusing. It is natural to answer a question when you are asked. However, stabbing pains in the head brings about a certain urgency in the response. Here you will find yourself sounding like a mad person just rambling off statements that have no substance.

The threats and punishment began each time that I walked through the doors of the church. I made it to each service. I was determined not to allow the cohorts of Satan to keep me away from learning about salvation through Jesus and the ways of holiness. Each Sunday, my punishment and spiritual violence far exceeded the previous Sundays. Every attempt that I made to serve the LORD was followed by some awful torture. Retribution was guaranteed.

There was also the torture that felt as though someone was ripping my teeth out with a pair of pliers. Not only did Satan want my church attendance to cease, he wanted to end my worship. I worshipped the LORD with a grateful heart. I worshipped with energy and gladness. I found great pleasure in worshipping. Satan wanted this to stop. He also wanted my heart to turn away from the LORD. He wanted me to become angry and blame the LORD. He needed my mind to turn away. I refused him.

Many of you are struggling in your attempt to spend time with the LORD. Some of you struggle over going into the house of the LORD due to this very torment that I am writing about. I urge you to continue going. It can be exasperating now. One day it will be rewarding. One day you will have peace of mind. You will not always be tormented like this. I know how it feels when Satan gives you an ultimatum: go to church and suffer, or leave the church and be left alone for the entire day. At the time of suffering this can be a hard choice to make, even when you love the LORD, especially when your attacks have been continual.

Satan will never let you go when you are serving the LORD. There is no need to cut deals with him. His deals are breakable and will always end in a disaster. Remember, a war has been waged against you. Since you are at war he will not willingly give you one day of peace. Any peace that you receive while in this spiritual war against Satan will be because of the grace of the Lord Jesus.

My advice to you is to go to the LORD's house and worship to the best of your ability every week. Stay focused on the LORD and not the people. It is important that you do not become sidetracked during this war. Claim victory over your mind. Speak out loud the biblical Word of the LORD even while in pain.

Never agree with Satan concerning your life. He is a liar and will never be honest concerning the LORD's word concerning you. You may feel as though the LORD is nonchalantly watching you go through this suffering. I assure you that he is not. I also understand that you have tried very hard to love the LORD through this pain. Keep going. I too have gone through this emotional rollercoaster. It has worked out for me and it will work out for you as well.

Allow me to encourage you. You are in training with the Holy Spirit. Decide to go through your training and succeed in reaching your expected end. You can do this the long way or the short way. You can go the easy route or the hard route. The LORD requires that you go through your training either way.

My advice is to take the short and easy route. Obey the Holy Spirit at all costs. He knows the path that you need to take to graduate from the school of the Holy Spirit. Satan and his dark angels can only attack you for a season. You will not be held in this spiritual headlock forever. Remember that the LORD is teaching you the ways of war through of his precious Holy Spirit.

You will make it! You will not struggle like this forever! You will get stronger every week! You will not always be possessed! There is liberty for you if you walk with the Holy Spirit. In due season you will be fully restored. I held on for dear mercy when I was going through my process. I made it and you can too.

I sat in a church listening to the prophet preach. He turned to me and said "You are holding on by a thread." At that time in my life, I was already feeling hopeless. I did not need a word from a prophet that brought no resolve. I needed hope. I realized that the Holy Spirit had been sent to comfort me and it was on him I would depend, not man.

The process of deliverance is ugly. During my training I learned most ministers do not want to deal with the truth of deliverance. They will touch on partial deliverance but not full deliverance. It takes a lifestyle of true sacrifice for a minister to walk in the necessary power to deliver someone. A life of consecration and remaining set apart is a must. A lifestyle of fasting and praying is a must. Remaining available to the LORD is a must. He will be second to none.

The Holy Spirit was not only my comforter, he was my friend. He removed me from my life of sin and wanted to use me to assist others. He said he would make me like Jesus. I liked the idea. Considering the suffering I had already endured I did not know if I would live through the process. Trustingly I gave up everything and decided to follow him.

During my suffering I searched for a reference. Had someone else lived through this type of torment? I decided to do some research. I read just about every book that I could about God's Word. I read every book that I could find concerning spiritual warfare. I had to get my hands on a book that would explain all of my suffering. I needed to know if someone had survived my kind of pain. I was not successful in my search. There were no books about my type of horrific demonic experiences. It appears no one had written books about this type of suffering, and I could fully understand why. They were probably institutionalized or in their graves.

Yet I continued in my search for helpful books. If it was a book about getting closer to Jesus I read it. Any help would do. This is when I came across a different war within my spirit. I thought that there was no harm in reading a simple book on the topic of Jesus. I learned that there was danger even here. While studying with the Holy Spirit it was revealed to me that unbelievers were writing books for the body of believers in Jesus. This has serious spiritual complications. After reading a book to get assistance against demonic spirits I found myself in a trance. I was taken up in the spirit while on the train headed into the city. I cried out and thought to myself, *Lord, give me a break already!* When the Holy Spirit rescued me from the trance he enlightened me. He informed me that prayer was necessary before reading any book. I needed wisdom to see if it was safe. Even books that seemed innocent.

The Holy Spirit taught me that spiritual things happen when you read books. Implications are made. Deposits are placed in your spirit and mind. Prayer should always precede the decision of whether to read a book. The Holy Spirit explained to me that my main sources of information were him and the Bible. There is also the matter of the individual who wrote the book. What type of spiritual practices does this individual participate in? Are there any spiritual battles afflicting him or her? What are their beliefs and lifestyle? Are there any curses placed upon their books? These are things that should be prayed about. Researching the life of the author is best.

Being the student that I was I continued getting into trouble. Me and my big ideas. I saw things differently than the Holy Spirit concerning strategy. I wanted to help him, so I did things my way. When I did the Holy Spirit was hard on me making me start all over again. He told me to do things the way that he told me the first time. The Holy Spirit had a strategy and technique that made sense only to him. I was to do it exactly that way

Being a woman, I felt that the LORD would have mercy upon me. He did not. He explained that Satan wouldn't have any mercy on me. He explained that if I wanted to walk in true and divine Holy Spirit power then I would have to learn how to follow complete instructions. I would have to walk through training like others before me.

Explaining to the Holy Spirit that this type of training was meant for a man did little good. He did not reply

Training changed my mindset concerning spiritual warfare as a woman. I remember crying to the LORD, expressing that my training in warfare was too hard. One-day silence took place after my outburst of sorrow. The lovely Holy Spirit said these words "You can cry, and I don't mind that you cry. It is what you do when you finish crying that concerns me." Then we went back to training and learning the Word of the LORD.

Eventually I stopped reminding the LORD that I was a woman. I stopped telling the Holy Spirit that this training was too hard for me. That was when the Holy Spirit taught me that Satan uses prophecy to manipulate the saints of the LORD. He explained that this was one of the tricky things concerning dark ministries that have a false face and witness of Jesus.

People are receiving a prophetic word that seems as though it is from the LORD because of its accuracy. Some claimed to minister a word for the LORDs glory, yet they were preaching against Jesus. The Holy Spirit began teaching me how to listen effectively to each message preached in its entirety before accepting it. He told me to reject "getting excited with the rising of the voice" coming from the pulpit. Listen to the words preached he said and open your heart and your mind. Figure out if the word is an anointed word from the LORD.

When I followed the instructions of the Holy Spirit I understood. I watched the crowd go crazy with excitement over something that had nothing to do with the Lord at all. It was not edifying but it was hypnotizing, and the music assisted greatly.

Listening effectively to messages being preached, I realized that in many cases they were not bible based lessons The LORD's children were being duped by a seducing spirit. Some were not as bold. They would use scriptures to back up their messages, but the character was always recognizable to me as wicked once the Holy Spirit revealed it.

The LORD needs his ministers to be set apart for his use alone. He needs them submissive and walking daily in the power and gifts of the Holy Spirit. He needs them to preach what he tells them to preach and not be enticed into teaching what is popular. As a up and coming minister of the gospel and deliverance minister in training, I urge you to teach the Word in season and out of season. Do not let your emotions get in the way. Do not allow yourself to be manipulated by the devil into saying what will draw the crowd. The LORD needs you to deliver his people and preach the unadulterated Gospel.

In the bible there is a book titled 2 Timothy. After reading chapter four, I learned that a time would come when people would not want to hear the truth of the LORDs word. They are more interested in learning fables. Learning fables can lead to idol worship and false god worship. This brings about spiritual oppression. We are in a season of spiritually dark oppression in the earth. Strong anointing's are necessary to destroy the yokes of every kind. There is a huge chance that the Holy Spirit wants to train and equip you for the task of setting the captives free. He would like to train you to walk in the ways of Jesus.

People will urge you to teach them their way. They will want to hear what is suitable for them. It is your job as a minister to teach what the LORD gives you to teach. In the bible there is a book titled Hebrews. While reading fourth chapter I learned of the strength of the LORDs word. I learned the effectiveness of the word and how important it is to read it, not taking It out of its context. Taking it out of context causes confusion for those whom are attempting to learn properly.

"The thief comes only to steal and kill and destroy; I have come that they may have life, and have it to the full" (John 10:10, NIV). The LORD wants to use us in his kingdom, to do a great work for him.

For us to be effective laborers in healing the sick and delivering the spiritually bound. There are requirements. We must understand biblical principles. We must be dedicated, submitted unto him and anointed. Your holy lifestyle will qualify you to penetrate the works of the evil one. Because you have chosen to be set apart, there will be special gifts available to you for Kingdom building and rescue missions in the supernatural. You will be anointed and have success in a love relationship with the LORD. There is a book in the bible titled Matthew. In the fifth chapter it explains how we should be as a light and an example to others. While being this exemplary light we should be active and not hidden away.

CHAPTER 23

POWER OF REBUKE

The Holy Spirit taught me that I had power. He always said this. He explained that he had to teach me how to use the power. I learned that I must speak the words he gave to me to make things manifest at the correct time.

I learned that timing was everything and that I had the power to speak to the demon in my life and make it flee. I was told that demons flee at the mention of Jesus's name. I tried it out one day. It did not work. I tried it on several occasions and it still did not work.

Since the Holy Spirit taught me that I had this authority over Satan and his cohorts, I wanted to use it. I was serious about my mission. I wanted to be free from the spiritual debt that was placed upon my life. With great boldness, I declared the blood of Jesus. There was no change and I remained vexed with demons. This took place for a long season in my life. I received rest by the grace of the Lord, but that was only for a short while. I had to get back to my training while under large amounts of distress and mental torment.

Finally, it was revealed unto me that there was something more to declaring the fleeing of a demon. The Holy spirit told me that I had to have power dwelling inside of me to see results. I seemed to have missed that part. I knew that I had power; I just had not received mine yet. During my training, I had not been filled with the power of the Holy Spirit because I was possessed. I was left possessed and had to fight through my demonic possession with a little grace and peace, here and there.

A person who is not being used by the Holy Spirit is not effective in the things of the Lord Jesus. The LORD desires to equip us to use his power to get his works done while we are here on this earth like Jesus did. Remember, it is his power that will work for his assignments. There are ministers of the gospel invoking other gods. They enchant demonic spirits. They rally with ancestral spirits all in the name of getting the Lord Jesus ministry work done. They become traitors to the divine gospel out of desperation. Their reasoning is because they have not received the gifts of the Holy Spirit. They go and seek out their own power in hopes that the LORD will bless it. Any healing done this way is not of the LORD. They will also bring about future danger for all involved. It is the Holy Spirit who will distribute the gifts. These individuals may not have waited patiently to be endowed with power. There is even the chance that they were not called to heal in the way they desired. The Father must be glorified not our flesh. Since they have gone about it to satisfy themselves they will pay a price for taking this route to receive divine powers. May the Holy Spirit lead them back. In Jesus name I pray, Amen.

I encourage you to read Acts 19:13–16 (NIV). If you take the time to read this book of the Bible, you will find that the man who attempted to cast out a demon from someone was attacked himself. Knowing the correct words to say is not the point. You must be filled with power from the LORD. Your life must be clean. Holy living is a necessity!

Since I learned that I needed the Holy Spirit's power to cast out the demons, there were some things that I needed to look at in my life. I began my checklist once again to see where I was in my walk of obedience. A holy lifestyle, a lifestyle of fasting and prayer, studying hard with the Holy Spirit, less complaining, and sitting with the Holy Spirit under his tutelage, on and on I went. There, my checklist was complete! I had not at this time been filled with the Holy Spirit. But at least I was on the right track to receiving this wonderful gift.

After much prayer, fasting, and supplication, I regained my ability to read my Bible properly. The words on the pages no longer moved about. I was now capable of understanding my biblical lessons. Those demons were indeed cast out. The works and sacrifice of Jesus released me from the demonic forces that had for, so many years tormented my soul. He also removed the demonic anointing that gave me access to what many called their third eye which was unknowingly implanted in my person when I was baptized into the cult, unknowingly. Finally, I had been made clean.

For those not aware of the term "third eye" there is more to this topic. It is an ungodly spiritual gift. It is not given from the Holy Spirit. It is instead a demonic spiritual access to and through you. You may have heard singers and rappers singing about their third eye. I had the third eye, and it is nothing to fool around with. Eventually this spirit being will destroy your life of peace.

It will destroy your life and anyone close to you it can be touched in a negative way. Satan plays for keeps. Those who have the third eye and are using it for financial and spiritual gain seem to be winning now. I desire to inform them that the winning streak won't last forever. They may have money and songs from this spirit being now, but in time this demon will turn on them.

The lifestyle won't last because eventually Satan will come to claim what is his. And the gifts that they've received by way of the third eye eventually will be used against them as a ransom for their souls. Satan's ultimate idea is to cause confusion in the lives of all who are around you, and then kill you. His goal is that you never learn or understand how much the LORD loves you and desires to give you his gifts.

CHAPTER 24

DELIVERANCE

I went through demonic oppression for a very long time. Although people prayed for me, healing did not present itself. Not until I went to the LORD for myself.

Surely the LORD uses his ministers in many facets. It is time for greater relationship and he is calling upon his children to do things differently. Many worship their pastors as if they are the LORD. In most cases this is not intentional, yet it naturally happens overtime if one is not careful.

Many ministry leaders place themselves upon pedestals, wanting to be recognized as great. They behave in such a manner to suggest they created heaven and earth themselves. The amount of adoration they expect is not healthy. As you grow in ministry it is important that you not get caught up in this behavior. Respect and honor your leaders. They are gifts to you from the LORD but do not use them as substitutes for getting to know the LORD and his Word for yourself.

This can happen if you are in a great Bible teaching ministry. In a teaching ministry, you can listen to the sermon and take notes. Once home, study all that you have learned to bring it into perspective. It is important to always ask the Holy Spirit to reveal what you need to know concerning the scriptures you are reading. Doing this daily will improve your growth and understanding of LORD's precious and Holy Word. Most of my healing took place in the privacy of my own home between me and the Holy Spirit.

The LORD knew that in times past I worshipped a religious man, teacher, idol, imam, a spiritual guide etc. I worshipped either a statue or cast stones to figure out what my day would be like. Since the LORD knew about my past idolatry it was necessary for me to depend solely upon him. It was because of this the Holy Spirit handled my healing in this manner.

He needed me to see that he sent Jesus as my answer. The power of his blood sacrifice for my sins was necessary to set me free. His walk of holiness. His lifestyle and character. He showed me that I would not need to give anyone the glory for my healing. All that I needed was him. During my intense suffering If someone had laid hands upon me, and I received healing somewhere deep down inside I may have looked at that person with great gratitude. The LORD did not want that for me. Not with my background of false god and idol worship.

In my case the LORD was my only option. Although the LORD uses his ministers to do his will, they do not determine whether you will be healed.

I have witnessed and experienced pastors using their authority to place fear in the heart of believers. They do this for self-gratification. They may tell you to give a certain amount of money to the LORD so that you can receive your healing. They may say it very convincingly and with great determination. For those able to be manipulated you will doubt receiving healing if you do not comply. Maybe the pastor wants you to do something you are not led of the Holy Spirit to do. I have heard some pastors say that out of disobedience to them certain people would lose the blessing received through their prayers. They believed that they were only blessed due to the pastor's prayers and not because the LORD loved them and desired to bless them. The sad thing was that the pastor was asking for unethical things. This my dear is bondage.

I have even seen pastors tell children of God that they will be cursed by God if they leave their church. I want you to understand that it is not disobedience to your leader if he is asking something unlawful or evil that gratifies them. Dear friend, this behavior is not of the LORD. Be a student of the word. Remain in right relationship with the LORD. In this way you will never be deceived. The Holy Spirit will not allow you to be.

Your deliverance comes from the LORD not a pastor, no matter how anointed he or she may be. All deliverance and healing come from the LORD. A minister is the vessel through which your healing may come. It is never the minister who has healed you.

CHAPTER 25

COMPASSION

I am stern when it comes to the Gospel of Jesus. For that I make no apologies. There is a set way that the LORD desires his kingdom to be run. Boldness in faith and taking no hostages when it comes to unclean spirits does not mean that I do not walk in love. Love is the key when it comes to ministry in all areas. I have a heart for those who are possessed with demonic spirits. I hate to see the LORD's precious ones living in bondage. Dear friend I have a request.

I request is that you show more love, support, and concern for those who are being delivered out of demonic oppression. It is important that they not be exposed and ridiculed during their time of helplessness. As you grow in ministry of the Gospel, be mindful of the aftermath that can take place once individuals are delivered. Their private lives have been exposed. The congregation may have witnessed them in indecent manners. This brings about another form of bondage if we are not careful. Be as a skilled surgeon and handle their matters as privately as possible. Deliverance should never be a sideshow or a main attraction.

These individuals don't need our abuse. What they do need is our support and prayer from everyone who is available. Possession is not a picnic in the park. Now while I ask you to show compassion and love toward them, it is important that you use Godly wisdom and discernment.

I say this because a person who has unclean spirits living inside of them can never be toyed with. They will use manipulation at any given moment to get their way. Showing love and kindness does not mean we should be gullible. We should pray diligently for them and as led by the Holy Spirit.

Always show compassion. Never reject them. Never discourage them from coming to church. They need to be in church! They need the LORD just as much as you and I. Ask yourself how Jesus would handle the situation? Would he put these people on blast and make them feel unwanted ? Would he make them feel unworthy of healing? I do not believe so.

King Jesus would pray for these individuals. He would show them compassion. He would never abuse them because he represents love. Dear friend, please intercede continually for your lost brothers and sisters. Maybe they haven't accepted Jesus into their lives yet. Maybe they do not believe in Jesus at all. Even so they need prayer and you are fit for the job.

While we're on this topic, let us make sure never to go against the individual. Let us instead go against the spirit that has taken control of this individual. It is not only the unsaved who are possibly demonically possessed. I have witnessed many regular church attenders who say they are saved and Holy Spirit filled but are demonically possessed. These possessed individuals form organizations against the pastor and the vision that God gave to him for the church. They confuse others. They gossip and lie. They slander the pastor and church family among many other things. With discernment from the Holy Spirit you will find possessed people from the pulpit to the parking lot.

Ushers are kingdom bodyguards against the kingdom of darkness. A non-Holy Spirit filled usher can be a target that satan can use. Many ushers are unaware that they are possessed. An usher is a perfect place for a demon to dwell in. In many churches, ushers are the greeters who welcome the children of the LORD as they walk through the doors of the church.

When an usher submits to the voice of Satan and mistreats a person, it blocks the message of love and Gospel coming from the pulpit. The usher is a defense line for the LORD against satan if Holy Spirit filled and discerning. Satan needs ushers as vessels to discourage prodigal sons and daughters from coming back to church. I recall times the Holy Spirit had to convince me to go back to a church where the usher was nasty and rude towards me.

It may be aggravating to watch the display of an individual with unclean spirits. Their many different behaviors will cause the minister delivering the message to become sidetracked. That is necessary if Satan is going to make the minister lose focus on the message of the gospels of Jesus and the prophets.

To help your brother or sister who is possessed, divert their negativity. Do not embrace it. When people come to you with gossip about the pastor or the ministry, don't give energy to it. Instead respond with the Word of the LORD. Tell them what the Bible states concerning the matter. Let them know that they should go and talk to the individual.

The way to affect people who are oppressed is to use the Word of the LORD and wisdom. Be discerning with the help of the Holy Spirit. Never allow them to dump drama on you and never engage in drama with them. Remain in control. Satan is a tricky foe. We must always use the LORD's Word as our final decision for everything. The Word of the LORD will cut through the lies of the enemy.

CHAPTER 26

DELIVERANCE

Never give up! Fight for your freedom from the oppression of evil spirits. If you are not one of those individuals who are instantly delivered from demons it can be a painful season to walk out. I share with you my testimony to encourage you while waiting for your deliverance.

Dear friend, if you have dealt with large amounts of spiritual darkness, it may take years of being faithful and obedient before experiencing deliverance. Understanding the strength that comes from reading Gods word will benefit you greatly. Never give up believing that you will be filled with the Holy Spirit and delivered from bondage. Inward hope will sustain you on those hard days filled with torment. Remain hopeful that you will be instantly delivered. It has happened for others and, so it will be with you. In Jesus name I declare it.

I pray that you remain faithful to a holy lifestyle. Do not beat yourself up over the decisions made that have oppressed you. Do not allow satan to discourage you in your walk of holiness. Be prepared for the schemes of satan. He attempts to make us feel as though we have not been delivered by causing us to doubt that we are the LORDs children. He is a manipulator. If possible, he will cause you to believe that you are one of his children because of being misunderstood by the church throughout your life. He uses this tactic to weaken your mind and faith in the LORD.

He will tell you that you don't belong in the church and manipulate you using false proof. These mental attacks can be discouraging in many ways. Especially when other children of the LORD are used as pawns to get his point across. This was one of the many things Beelzebub said to me. He tried to get me to stop seeking the LORD. Beelzebub tried to convince me that I would never be free from his clenched hands. If it had not been for the Holy Spirit's encouragement I would have believed him.

Another form of discouragement began oppressing me. Witnessing others be healed and delivered instantly left me feeling ignored. My mind processed the LORD's awareness of my suffering. It also processed that the there was no way that he could love me if he allowed me to suffer in this way.

Dear friend, there will be times when you are too exhausted for a spiritual fight with demons. Spiritual warfare is strategic, and it takes a strong mind to endure. During this time, the Holy Spirit encouraged me to shut down from all extracurricular activities. He wanted me to be prepared for the battle. During this time, I fasted and prayed to tame my flesh. After each session of this intense strategy of training with the Holy Spirit, I was given rest.

Once in this place of rest, the Holy Spirit fought my battles for me. I had already done my part. The LORD sent angles of war to do battle against the very demons that had oppressed me. He will do the same for you. I am one who wanted and wished well for everyone, with or without them knowing about it. I was a cheerleader for the people. I wanted to see others do well. I desired and prayed that others would walk in blissful relationship with the Holy Spirit. Over a period of many years of oppression, my attitude changed. I no longer cared whether someone was healed. In fact, I was angry when others were healed in my home church. I was angry because I was waiting patiently for my healing and I hadn't received it.

The Holy Spirit saw this change in me and did not like it. This change brought about a distasteful, selfishness and disobedient attitude. The Holy Spirit warned me that I was coveting my brother's gift of deliverance. He saw that I was still holding on to my past. I was still a self-righteous sinner who silently and within my heart bragged about how much I followed the laws. In fact, I was still an idol worshipper. Honestly, I was still a very judgmental person who thought that I deserved liberation because of how good I had been.

As the Holy Spirit ministered to my heart concerning my behavior, I did some self-seeking. I had to be honest with myself. I was not looking at the grace of the LORD. I was unable to accept the grace of the LORD due to all my good works. Within my own mind, I was a good girl and deserved to be healed. I followed the commandments, therefore I deserved to be healed.

I was taken by surprise when the Holy Spirit revealed to me that I would not be healed until I had learned my lesson. This may be the case with you as well. There may be some areas that he wants you to grow in before you receive complete deliverance.

During this time, I observed others being healed from the very things which I had been praying for deliverance from. There was a time when demons that were cast out of another individual entered my body. It was unfortunate that I became an open vessel where demons could lodge both comfortably and quietly. This was insulting to me and I became bitter. Once I allowed the bitterness to dwell within my heart, it was hardened.

One Sunday a married couple came to the church where I was a member. The wife expressed openly that she needed deliverance. Her husband confirmed that many demons were attacking her. They both stated that they had been seeking deliverance for her for many years and were not successful. They said that they were told of the church by a friend and decided to visit. They wanted to see if the wife could receive deliverance from the demons taunting her.

Once the apostle prayed for her she was visibly better almost instantaneously. The apostle asked the ushers to assist the woman off the floor and she was given some water. This was the end of her demonic trouble. The following week the woman came back to church and said that her life and health had changed drastically. She and her husband joined the church.

I watched the woman come to church for weeks at a time and she always seemed to be in a lasting state of total peace. Viewing this woman having such peace brought about within myself bitter sweet emotions. I was hurting because the demons that left that woman left her and came to dwell inside of me.

I recall the communication that took place between her demons and mine on the day that she was delivered. Once the demons knew they were being cast out they began seeking a place to go. The demons began to communicate through the church seeking shelter. It was then that the demons lodged inside of me said to the demons lodged inside of her, "You can come here".

I could not speak openly because service was going on but I immediately spoke silently within myself to the demons saying, *Oh no, you can't*, and I called upon the Holy Spirit for help. My Apostle looked directly at me when it was happening. He knew what was taking place but at the time was not able to intervene for reasons I do not know.

The Apostle just cast the demon out of the woman and they came directly into me. I was at a loss for words. I was confused about how this whole ministry thing was supposed to operate. I was frustrated with the LORD. I said to the LORD, do you mean to show me that it did not take a whole lot for her, but you are letting me sit here in this very ministry and suffer? Do you mean to allow me to witness a simple deliverance, but you won't deliver me, and I am your child as well? I was both sad and furious. Moreover, I now had more demons lodged inside of me.

It was then that the lovely Holy Spirit dealt with my heart and mind concerning his ways. He shared the wisdom of the LORD with me, and I began to learn. The Holy Spirit taught me the next level of understanding the LORD's love and grace. He also taught me that instead of looking at the woman while she was being delivered, I should have been in prayer and a personal worship time with him. Therefore, I was exposed and became an open vessel.

During the time of the woman's deliverance, I silently expressed feelings of jealousy and envy. I was wishing that it was me and selfishness came in. This caused me to be susceptible and the enemy Satan used it against me. Therefore, I was chosen as a house for these demons and others were not. My heart needed to be pure during the time of the deliverance and mine was not. My desperation made sure of it.

He explained to me that instead of wishing that it was me whom was being healed, I should have been looking at how lovely it was that this woman would be well again and in her right mind. The Holy Spirit said to me that instead of being sad I should be giving the LORD glory for blessing my sister in the LORD for the blessing of healing that she had received.

Once the LORD's wisdom was introduced to my heart, I had to decide whether to receive it. Once I received it, I reevaluated my behavior. It was then that I learned some things. I learned some lessons. I also began to understand his keeping power. I began to recognize how the Holy Spirit can sustain me until the set time of my healing. I realized that although my situation did not feel good to my person, patients was still required. I was to be patient and wait until the LORD saw fit to bring total restoration into my life.

It was in this season of my life that I learned a huge lesson which was, my works did not impress the LORD nor was my healing going to be determined by how good I was. Once I came to this realization I understood that it did not matter that I was such a good person who gave a lot to the needy. The LORD was seeking an obedient heart and not an obedient purse or wallet.

Divine healing is both available and free to all who believe! Sure, healing comes in different ways, but it is still healing nonetheless.

I realized that it didn't matter if I worked hard. It didn't matter if I gave a lot financially either. What did matter to the LORD was that I had accepted Jesus as my Lord and Savior and that I trusted him. It mattered that I was willing to be used of the LORD. It mattered that I would not allow the temptations of this world to take me away from an obedient path and that I was faithful and would remain faithful until the end, not just until I had received my healing. It mattered that I would not look at my works as a reason why I was healed. These are some of the things that the Holy Spirit wanted me to understand. It was about me being available and a light that was willing to shine in darkness.

During this time of suffering there were some things that gave me hope. One of them was that I knew that eventually I would be healed. I was sure of this because of the promise that was given unto me according to the word of the LORD. Jesus had died on the cross at Calvary and the shedding of his blood redeemed my soul as well as provided a healing for me if I believed. I did believe. When the Father in heaven saw me, he did not see the filthy person that my actions had caused me to become. What he did see was the Lord and the sacrifice that was made on my behalf and on yours.

The word of the LORD revealed it to me, my heart confirmed for me and by faith it was already done. In due season, every devouring and unclean spirit that had connected itself to me had to leave. It was important to the Holy Spirit that I remembered that I was not healed because I was a great person or because of the things that I accomplished on behalf of his kingdom. He needed me to understand and to never forget that that healing that came to me was a gift from Jesus and that it was a gift to the children of the LORD. It cannot be purchased.

During my season of training with the Holy Spirit I learned about loving the LORD. I began to understand the necessity of obedience. I learned that out of love, obedience takes place. Obedience should not be something that I do because I desire something from the LORD. I should seek after the LORDs heart out of a pure motive alone. During this time, I received an understanding of the LORD's love. It helped me a lot. I realized that he loved me and that he desired that I be made whole. I also learned that the LORDs love for me was sincere and he did not have to rush to my aide to prove his love for me. He moves in his own timing, not when I felt an emergency was at hand.

I realized that when he moved in his own timing it wasn't that he was ignoring me or being mean. I learned that he had a plan and strategy in action for my life. He was working on my issues. I was not always able to see him working but he was. It was then that my fear was conquered. I knew that I would not be sick for the rest of my life. I learned how to hold on to my promise of healing and to do so in faith.

Through my battles I learned to endure. Gaining wisdom, I ceased beating myself up and trying to prove to the LORD that I was worthy of the healing. I learned that God's grace was a gift and that there was no amount of money that I could pay to receive it. I only needed to trust in him. The LORD loves me, and he loves you too. That, my friend is final. Finally, I concluded that I was not in control.

The LORD would do this miracle deliverance for me in his perfect timing. I concluded that my lack of deliverance was not a punishment but a process. This process was necessary for me to go through so I could help someone else. I released myself from this self-torture and decided to let go. I let the LORD deliver me from the torment and harassment of dark angels in his perfect timing. I decided to praise him despite my suffering. The lesson of selflessness and sacrifice while in suffering was one of the most important lessons learned.

Beloved please read and digest this next point of mine very seriously. Allow it to be embedded into your heart for a later season of your life, if not now. It is important that you understand it doesn't matter what kind of rituals, chants, or dark spiritual practices you've done in your past. It doesn't even matter how many candles you've burned to appease the idols you've worshipped. It does not matter how many sacrifices you have made. The LORD desires to form a relationship with you. He loves you more than you will ever understand.

My dear, you could have offered a million sacrifices to the devil, and it would never change the LORD's mind about loving you. It would never change his mind about wanting you back home and in a right relationship with him. He understands more than you think that he does. He knows that you have been manipulated, hurt, and confused about where you belong spiritually. He knows that Satan has maneuvered his way into your life. He wants to forgive you and bring you back into a healthy and intimate relationship with him.

My dear, you may have cut and mutilated yourself until you bleed all over the floor and this will not change his mind about you. Salvation is still available to you. It doesn't matter how much witchcraft you have done. Sure, the LORD does not like this behavior, but he understands that you were ignorant to the schemes of satan. Although your past may have spiritual consequences, it is still behind you. Today, you can make better decisions. You can decide to stop these detestable practices now. Repent by turning away from them forever. The LORD is ready and willing forgive you when you do! He wants to forgive you. He loves you dearly and he wants you to come back to him. He desires that you join the rest of his children and live in harmony in the earth while working in his kingdom doing kingdom minded things.

The LORD is waiting for you with open arms. For those of you who are suffering with torment the LORD holds your solution. He is a bondage breaker. There is no bondage that can ever defeat him. Many are caught in a web of lies and deceit. Witchcraft has been placed over their lives. You find yourself stuck in cycle of destruction. Many of you have been so disastrously affected by witchcraft that you now embrace self-sabotage. This is because of what was done to your mind while this curse was placed upon you. Many of you are assisting the enemy in your own destruction. Satan no longer needs to speak badly about your life because you are doing it for him. He no longer needs to speak subliminally to you through your subconscious mind and into your spirit. He has trained you very well on how to do it for him.

Now you find yourself repeating negativity into your own mind which then transfers into your spirit. Demons no longer need to assist you in this process. You will fail on your own every single time. With the assistance of the LORD, this self-sabotage can be eliminated. You can be restored from subliminal brainwashing. He desires to rescue you from Satan's grasp. He also desires to rescue you from yourself. The adversary has influenced someone to touch your life with witchcraft. He or she has manipulated the Word of the LORD or used some age-old ritual to condemn your spirit man into bondage, and now you and your entire household are suffering.

My advice to you is to focus on the Word of the LORD. Live a life that is pleasing in his sight and begin embracing the ways of holiness that will eventually bring you into an intimate relationship with him. The LORD is the one who holds your deliverance from spiritual darkness. It is my prayer that your reading this book will allow you to avoid making the many mistakes that I did. This should cause your road to recovery to go much smoother.

Oh, how I wished that someone had prepared me for a battle such as this. My struggles with being a believer in Jesus was much different than it was in the past. This time around I experienced sitting in churches where pastors and prophets claimed that they alone held the key to my deliverance. Rarely did I ever hear them exalt the LORD, mainly themselves. In their boasting they shared with the congregation that they would release the healing as they please. It had to be spoken out of their mouth.

There are some who claim to be ministers of the gospel who operate their ministries as witches and warlocks would. These false ministers use biblical scripture in their teaching to hide the truth of their intent which is to lock away both your spirit and your Godly purpose. Whether they are deliberately using witchcraft techniques or not is not the question. What they are doing is wrong. They are not going about things according to biblical scripture. Anytime things are done outside of the ways of the LORD, there is room for error.

The Holy Spirit allowed me to experience fear of church leadership for a long season. At the end of the season he trained me to be bold and discern what healthy leadership looks like. Any leadership acting outside of what is pleasing to the LORD was out of order. There was no need for me to fear them. Once I began to understand, fear was removed. I no longer feared leadership but respected and properly honor ministers of the gospel.

These false ministers will go to any extent to reach your inner spirit man. They will use prayer chants as a way of controlling the minds of the innocent congregation. It is sad that they mistreat the flock that they vowed to care for, teach and protect. Since they have dealt unjustly toward their congregations the LORD will deal justly with them.

Witchcraft is a means of using manipulation to get one's own way over an individual or situation. Witches or warlocks many times use prayer and scripture as magicians use magical powers obtained from Lucifer to influence or fascinate. Many have been manipulated by magicians who pretend to be ministers. It is easier for these magicians to manipulate the masses when they do so within the walls of a church or ministry. It is less noticeable. Most people let their guards down in the house of the LORD. They are most vulnerable there because they believe the best about those who bear the title of a minister.

Today witches and warlocks are holding their services within the walls of churches. The cross is used as trickery to draw the innocent and ignorant. Pay close attention to what is being taught from the pulpit. Read along during service. We must read the word of the LORD often. Doing so will help us understand exactly what we have just agreed with when we state "amen" after the sermon.

What are you agreeing to? Have you thought about the implications of your agreement? What have you allowed your spirit to agree with that has bound you up to this day? Please think about what you have just read. If you have agreed with a wizard who calls himself a pastor, or a witch who calls herself a pastor, repent and ask the Holy Spirit to help you remove the curse. The Holy Spirit will help you get on the correct path. Jesus is waiting for you, and the Holy Spirit is ready to train you in the LORD's army on how to defend yourself from future traps of the devil.

Allow me to share with you another form of deception that leads to the bondage of an individual. Spiritual cleansing baths have become a form of manipulation for many individuals who have come to me for assistance. Allow me to share my personal experience concerning spiritual baths. I have never experienced a spiritual bath in the physical realm but in the spirit realm I have. This took place long ago when I was taken up in the spirit by two demonic spirits. When I was taken up these demons did with me as they pleased.

It is the Holy Spirit who has assisted me in the deliverance process of those who have had these types of rituals performed on them. It is unfortunate that these rituals cause such horrible mental tortures. Allow me to give the example of the bondage of spiritual baths. A spiritual bath is an evil cleansing and baptism of wickedness. I understand that this may seem to be an oxymoron because the word cleanse makes people believe that they will be cleansed of something dirty or negative, when in fact the opposite is happening.

Over time it has been proven that Lucifer attempts to take things that are holy and tarnishes them. He takes that which is holy and pollutes it causing it to become toxic and unfit for use. As believers we are baptized into the kingdom of the LORD. It is true that a person can be baptized into Satan's kingdom. Which is the kingdom of darkness. If someone is seeking a life of righteousness but naively receives a spiritual bath they will find themselves in a dark place spiritually

For those who are very aware that they are taking a spiritual bath they will be held responsible. Then there are those who have physical ailments and have been lied to concerning spiritual baths. They believe that they are doing something healthy for their body. There are those who take the baths because they were told that it will help their, spirit, soul, skin, and intimacy into the spiritual realm with their creator. It is sad that when these individuals realize that this is not the case, they are in a space of torment and spiritual darkness.

When I share with you concerning spiritual baths, I am referring to the ritualistic anointing of oils and herbs that some use as a form of healing or connecting to a certain spirit realm to enhance relationships, understanding, or influence in the spirit realm. Water is used, either heated or not, but people are treated by being immersed in water.

These ritual baths may or may not be accompanied by prayer or the speaking of quotes. Oils that have been previously prayed over may be used. There are different ways in which an individual can have a spiritual bath. I share these details with you hoping to give you an idea of how this idea may be presented to you.

Many believers in the kingdom of the LORD are baptized into water to express their dedication to the LORD. They do so in the name of the Father, Son, and Holy Spirit. For the believer in the LORD any other spiritual baptism is not of the LORD and must be avoided.

Through the counseling of others, I have learned to understand the wicked outcome of spiritual baths. A satanic baptism, is the best way for me to express it. Victims of this bath have come to me afterwards, expressing their expectations from the bath. They were supposed to be cleansed from trauma, illness, toxic and emotional pain. Instead these individuals found themselves in the darkness of trouble in spiritual realms. The outcome was that they became filthy and possessed by demons.

The words "spiritual bath" suggest that one is receiving something holy and cleansing. In truth, this bath causes the individual to become more spiritually sensitive to the touch and actions of satan and those within his kingdom. He is better able to connect with a person when they are baptized into his kingdom. This baptism is a form of submission and allows the torment to become greater over time.

A spiritual bath will bring about an evil immersion. Satan connects to individuals in subtle ways. The individual will not receive a holy connection to the Creator of the universe once this practice is completed. The spirit realm opens to this individual in many ways. Since this is of the devil the results are always negative. Most often during this process, the chakras and solar plexus of an individual are opened. The persons spirit man opens like a vortex and satan and his team of demons come through and connect with the individual as they desire, which will be quite often.

People have contacted me for assistance after receiving spiritual baths. In most cases the individual has lost their natural minds by the time they come to me. Deliverance is necessary by this time and it can be such a tedious process that most individuals feel so overwhelmed and frustrated that they desire to give up rather than fight. Once the individual shows signs of unwillingness to fight back effectively, demons come in full attack. Demons take advantage of this exhausted individual. Demons then begin to remind the individuals of their past failures which hinders their deliverance.

These demons send negative and self-harming ideas to the individual subliminally. They telepathically and audibly speak into the individuals mind. Demons on this level assignment of torment can type their demonic messages into individual's minds by way of tapping in certain positions on the head. Like one types using a keyboard. It is a form of demonic hypnotizing. The individual will receive the message internally when it is tapped into the mind. In this way they abuse their victims physically and spiritually. Over time the individual finds fighting to be too much of a struggle and decides that it is easier to stay demonically oppressed and go along with the pain and suffering, than to remove themselves.

This way of thinking results in self-defeating behavior. It is embedded into the mind of the individual. From that point the individual is conditioned into obsessing over the suffering that will overtake them if they attempt to leave. Through this self-defeating subliminal messaging sent from the devil, the individuals are mentally conditioned to believe they are not strong enough to leave their situation. They are manipulated into believing their best option is to submit.

The feeling of guilt is another weapon that satan and his demons use against these mentally tormented individuals. Once an individual gains boldness they decide to leave their situation despite the cost. It is at this place that they find themselves strong enough to disassociate from the demons. The demons then change their approach and become both rescuer and abuser to the individual. At this point, feelings of obligation to the demons begin to present themselves. The average person does not see this coming. Along with this feeling of obligation comes guilt. Once these emotions begin to manifest, confusion is not far behind.

These feelings are hard to ignore. The enemy taunts a person with false revelation. Demons are strategic and will convince the person that they were merciful unto them. It is unbelievable that this works on a person desperately trying to escape their torment but unfortunately it does. It is mental manipulation.

What causes the confusion is the scheme satan uses where demons become both abuser and rescuer. This causes them to be viewed as authoritative figures in their lives. They become substitute gods. They pretend to show mercy when the LORD decides not to, for whatever reason. They do this by removing the torment, pretending to be merciful and caring. When an individual has waited and prayed to the LORD for mercy from demonic torment and receives it not, but a demon comes along and although it is the one causing suffering, it also gives mercy, the desperate individual accepts its assistance and often submits all over again.

It is common for these demons to become as family to these individuals. Reason being, they are the ones who determine the peace and happiness of their captured vessels. These demons have reached deep into the heart chambers of these broken individuals. They have even been able to cause them to feel guilty for wanting them to be cast out.

The longer the spirits have been connected to a person determines how well they have gotten to know them. The length or familiarity with the person gives them a huge advantage. They study them intensively in order that they will understand them both completely. They know what makes the person tick. They are aware of the needs of the person as well as what they need to feel complete.

To be effective in defeating these demons, it is important for the tormented individual to understand that they do not need the demons but that the demons need them. This is where the mind game gets tricky. A person must know who they are and where they truly belong. They must understand and remember their goal is to be with the LORD. Demons cannot afford for their tormented victim to understand this.

Many leave the spiritual bath with a chemical imbalance and legions of demons living inside them. When people receive spiritual baths, they allow false ministers of the Gospel, ministers of Lucifer, mystics, or spiritualists to bathe them in oils and place cloths upon their body. Like when a minister of the Gospel anoints one with oil and them a prayer cloth. It can be so familiar and peaceful that they may not question the pros and cons of receiving the cloth.

Remember, taking this cloth is your way of accepting all that comes with it. Be mindful of who you are receiving anointed or spiritual handkerchiefs from. If you are uncomfortable taking the handkerchief, do not allow it to be embraced. Meaning, do not take it, simply say no but thank you anyway. If you are uncomfortable receiving prayer from an individual you should refuse that as well, at least until you are sure of the person's motives and comfortable receiving the prayer. This is your life and health. You have the right to deny any form of deliverance or prayer that you do not feel is right for you.

You are responsible for the care of your soul. Never allow anyone to place their praying hands upon your head or body without your permission. If someone does this to you reject their prayers. You have the right to rebuke this individual. Do not be fearful of them. At the same time do not be rude, out of order or distracting. Be mindful that you are responsible for protecting yourself from evil spiritual transactions that may take place in the form of prayer and the laying on of hands. If you desire, for the sake of not making a scene, you can rebuke them silently.

The LORD and his lovely Holy Spirit will back you up in the spiritual realm. Once this is done, walk out of that church immediately and do not look back, unless you learn that there has been a change in that church or the LORD has sent you there.

Some may fear offending a pastor by asking a question. In most cases, it is normal because we hold pastors in such high regard. After all, we are not in such an authoritative position and surly feel powerless in a situation like this. Be prayerful and ask the Holy Spirit for assistance in sharing your concerns. Many individuals are broken and distressed in life and are willing to try anything. It is unfortunate that this very attitude and lack of self-assurance causes them to be vulnerable to spiritually abusive ministers who claim to teach the gospel but truly minister mysticism.

Once the bath has been completed and all the ritualistic verses and quotes have been said, it is a done deal. A toxic spiritual realm is ready to embrace you. From this point the individual becomes a living mess, much like I was before I was returned home by the lovely Holy Spirit and rededicated my life to Jesus.

I am amazed at the foolish behavior portrayed when we do not allow the word of the LORD to guide us. When our thoughts are cloudy our decision making can be horrible. Believe me when I say that I am not being judgmental. I am right here with you. Believe me, I get it and have done it! We can get set free from the evil of satan and go right back into another one of his traps. I have had several people come to me for deliverance from witchcraft, they get delivered and you will find them going right back to the place where they were manipulated into the witchcraft to begin with. The next time the trap is different yet still the same.

Some people accepted spiritual baths and when they became possessed by demons, they attempted to get help from the very individuals who caused them to become possessed in the first place. One individual contacted the person back because they believed their spiritual bath went wrong because they began hearing voices. They were told that they would begin hearing the LORD or their ancestors. What they did hear were the violent voices of controlling and manipulative demons.

In one case, the mystic minister said that they would resolve the problem if they came back. When they did, they watched as he attempted to correct the wrong. Nothing changed in their condition and they were asked to come again on another day. When they came back, the ritual ended in failure and the mystic minister became belligerent and insisted that they leave and never to come back. He also informed them that they were to never contact him ever again concerning the matter.

On another occasion an individual went back to the spiritualist for her condition to be fixed but after the chants, her condition worsened. The voices got louder and more violent. Eventually the spiritualist gave up and said that he could do no more. To add insult to injury, this spiritualist charged the woman more money, despite the outcome. She was horrifically affected by this deceit. This happened to her all because she has heard of some new thing called a spiritual bath and she figured that it would help ease her troubles.

WARNING!

Please, for your own sake do not seek assistance from the people who have infected you. Go to a church that is a Bible-based deliverance ministry. It is unfortunate but many churches refuse to deal with the topic of demons. Many do not even believe in demons. For those who do believe in demons but refuse to deal with them, you will probably be asked to leave their church if you are full of them. Since this is the case, do your research on the ministry that you are considering going to before going. I would hate for you to suffer any more than you already have. You have been through enough.

It is important to find a church that is Bible based, healthy, and anointed of the LORD. The fruit of the Spirit should be evident. You will need to test the ministry to see if it is the LORDs church. Avoid the spiritual bondage that comes from connecting with ungodly ministries.

Remember, you have the right to deny any form of deliverance or prayer that you feel is not right for you. This is your body and the LORD expects you to take care of it. Some of the spiritual bondage that I went through was because I would not stick up for myself due to fear and intimidation of leadership. I did not want to seem disrespectful to a man of woman of the LORD.

I suffered in much bondage due to my lack of wisdom concerning how to handle my issues with leadership properly. It was not until the Holy Spirit taught me that he would not fight anything for me that I could stop on my own. He taught me that I had to be bold, open my mouth and stick up for myself when I am being wronged in the church.

He would not fight for me when I was unwilling to fight for myself. I was fearful of hurting someone's feelings, being considered ungodly. I was fearful of wrongfully judging as well. I was hurt in the church many times and did not want to be the one who was now causing other people pain. Satan knew this about me and he used my love for the people of God against me.

I learned the hard way not to worry about hurting the feelings of someone when the price was my possible bondage. The Holy Spirit allowed me to be bound up spiritually until I spoke out and said, "No!" "No, I will not come to your conference out of obligation just because you asked me. No, I will not receive your prayer and laying on of hands upon my head, so that you are not embarrassed before the congregation. No, no, no more! I will no longer receive prayers that I feel uncomfortable with. I also stopped saying amen to prayers without fully understanding all of what was being said. It was then that the LORD stepped in and fought many mighty battle on my behalf. It all began with me opening my mouth in wisdom.

CHAPTER 27

SATAN WANTS OUR CHILDREN

The Great I Am has entrusted us with his beloved children. We are their keeper and responsible earthly guardian. We must be sure to teach our children of the biblical Jesus. We must explain the importance of being obedient unto the LORD. It is crucial that this be taught at a young age. We must not wait until we feel that it is time, we must begin sharing this wisdom key from the time of conception. Likewise, we must be living examples of this obedience.

I believe, if I had learned of biblical scripture and the importance of holiness as a child, I could have bypassed a lot of the spiritual bondage that I went through. If we don't teach our children about the LORD, biblically, we are leaving satan to the task. We can be assured that he will not teach them of anything that is holy.

Unless we steer the way, our children will learn of higher power that is not Adonai our LORD. Let us make a commitment to be diligent in our teachings of Jesus Christ who died on the cross so that our sins could be redeemed. Let us strive to be a light in a world that has become darkened with sin.

Let us always remember that our children are not only listening to us, but they are also watching our behavior. They watch us walk our faith out daily. Since we can learn from our mistakes, we should review our behavior daily. During this self-review one of the questions that we should ask ourselves is what am I showing my children.

Are we showing our children that life's struggles will not determine our obedience unto the LORD? Do we show our children that nothing will stop us from living a life that is pleasing to the LORD? Please take some time to think about it.

Do we show our children that we will walk strongly in our faith and not stray from the path of righteousness? If we cannot pay a bill, do we go to the extreme point of doing things that are not pleasing unto the LORD?

Are horoscopes being read to determine the outcome of our day? Are we watching television programs that invite spiritual bondage into our homes, all in the name of "just a little entertainment?"

Our actions help our children make good decisions. We are the ones who show them the benefits of not serving other gods when the opportunity arises. Realize that under such a season of the power of influence, our children need a way to escape if peer pressure tries to tempt them to walk away from the LORD. Practice scenarios that may come to them when they are out and about in the community. This type of role play could save their life one day.

Share the gospel of Jesus with your children in a fun and effective way. It is best to begin while they are young. Make sharing the gospel relevant to the time that they are living. In doing so your child will be able to stand up to spiritual bullies who will tell them that the Bible is old fashioned and unnecessary. Teach them to steer clear of those who say that holiness is a lifestyle of the past. Assist your child with gaining wisdom. If you do so your child will make better decisions when temptation comes their way. Biblical wisdom is key. May the lovely Holy Spirit be with you in your daily walk of holiness and in the training of your children.

Although healing is free and a gift from the LORD, be diligent in the support of kingdom building through the ministry that you have been assigned to. We should support our assigned ministry both in finance and in action. A lot goes into running a successful ministry that will glorify our LORD. There are monthly expenses that must be paid such as electricity and water. More than likely there are toiletries in the restroom, for our, convince. These necessities are often over looked but if they were not made available to us we would more than likely notice right away. Some would probably even complain.

Most ministries are not debt free and paid and full. The average ministry pays a monthly rent or a mortgage. More than likely there are several fun and enlightening programs that your leadership would like to implement for the members benefit. Remember, these things cost money. Crayons and coloring books may be part of the curriculum to assist in learning. Bibles and study guides for the youth may be needed. It takes a lot to run a Godly and successful ministry. The Pastor cannot do it all on his or her own. When giving, be sure to give with a cheerful heart. This is what causes our LORD to be glad. Most of us desire to give to the LORD house with a glad heart which is quite lovely.

We should pray for wisdom against manipulation and abuse in the house of God. Never allow bad experiences to remove you from the body of believers. Ungodly behavior does not represent the LORD. Poor behavior does not represent the church.

Now would be a great time to begin making the necessary changes in your life. It may be a good idea to keep in mind all that you have learned while reading this book. If you are in spiritual bondage, your healing is on the way. Let me remind you that once you receive your healing is it important that you refrain from committing sinful acts. If you choose not to listen and decide to continue in your sin, you will become sick again, it is only a matter of time. Keep in mind that demonic spirits are waiting for you to slip back into the lifestyle that you have been delivered from. They will be waiting to consume you if you slip up. Your actions will have given them the legal right to do so. A holy lifestyle is very important for a successful outcome.

May the Holy Spirit guide you through every decision that you make. In Jesus's mighty name, Amen.

Mattia Lajuan Harris is a student of the precious Holy Spirit and delights in the beauty of worship. She is trained in deliverance and healing. Mattia studies Psychology, Theology, and Liberal arts at Mercer University in Atlanta Georgia. In her free time, she enjoys writing songs, drawing, painting, making jewelry and is currently learning how to sew. Mattia has been called of the LORD to set the captives free.

Journal Your Experiences Here

Journal Your Experiences Here

Journal Your Experiences Here

Journal Your Experiences Here

Journal Your Experiences Here

Journal Your Experiences Here

Journal Your Experiences Here

Journal Your Experiences Here

Journal Your Experiences Here

Journal Your Experiences Here

Journal Your Experiences Here

Journal Your Experiences Here

Journal Your Experiences Here

Journal Your Experiences Here

Journal Your Experiences Here

Journal Your Experiences Here

Journal Your Experiences Here

Journal Your Experiences Here

Journal Your Experiences Here

Journal Your Experiences Here

Journal Your Experiences Here

Journal Your Experiences Here

Journal Your Experiences Here

Journal Your Experiences Here

Journal Your Experiences Here

Journal Your Experiences Here

Journal Your Experiences Here

Journal Your Experiences Here

Journal Your Experiences Here

Journal Your Experiences Here

Journal Your Experiences Here

Journal Your Experiences Here

Journal Your Experiences Here

Journal Your Experiences Here

Journal Your Experiences Here

Journal Your Experiences Here

Journal Your Experiences Here

Journal Your Experiences Here

Journal Your Experiences Here

Journal Your Experiences Here

Journal Your Experiences Here

Journal Your Experiences Here

Journal Your Experiences Here

Journal Your Experiences Here

Journal Your Experiences Here

Journal Your Experiences Here

Journal Your Experiences Here

Journal Your Experiences Here

Journal Your Experiences Here

Journal Your Experiences Here

Journal Your Experiences Here

Journal Your Experiences Here

Journal Your Experiences Here

Journal Your Experiences Here

Journal Your Experiences Here

Journal Your Experiences Here

Journal Your Experiences Here

Journal Your Experiences Here

Journal Your Experiences Here

Journal Your Experiences Here

Journal Your Experiences Here

Journal Your Experiences Here

Journal Your Experiences Here

Journal Your Experiences Here

Journal Your Experiences Here

Journal Your Experiences Here

Journal Your Experiences Here

Journal Your Experiences Here

Journal Your Experiences Here

Journal Your Experiences Here

Journal Your Experiences Here

Journal Your Experiences Here

Journal Your Experiences Here

Journal Your Experiences Here

Printed in the United States
By Bookmasters